Your Mental Health Questions Answered

By

J. Lucy Boyd, RN, BSN

Your Mental Health Questions Answered

By J. Lucy Boyd, RN, BSN

July 2011   First Edition

Copyright 2011 by J. Lucy Boyd

All Rights Reserved

Big Apple Publishing Company. Inquiries welcome.

Lucy@JLucyBoyd.com

Disclaimer

"Your Mental Health Questions Answered" is meant to
increase your interest in mental health topics. It is not
designed for self-diagnosis or the diagnosis of others and is
not meant to substitute for professional advice. See a
physician or mental health professional for any psychological
concerns. The author, contributors, publishing companies and
other agents are not liable for any consequences related to the
reading of this book, and they do not make any warranty,
express or implied, regarding the contents of the book.

Acknowledgements

First and foremost, I must thank the psychiatrists: Marcia Sirota, MD, Samuel Mowerman, MD, Carole Lieberman, MD, Leon Hoffman, MD, Nzinga Harrison, MD and Madeleine M. Castellanos, MD; and psychologists: Mentwab Wuhib, PhD, Tina B. Tessina, PhD, Ashley L. Solomon, PsyD, Karen Sherman, PhD, Simon A. Rego, PsyD, Steve Orma, PsyD, Ronald L. Mann, PhD, Gary W. Lewandowski, Jr., PhD, Aimee Kotrba, PhD, Joann Paley Galst, PhD, Jennifer L. Fee, PsyD, Patricia Farrell, PhD, Matthew Clark, PsyD and Jeffrey L. Brown, PsyD who each made an invaluable contribution to this ambitious project.

I also send a big thank you to Jake Lynn at the American Psychoanalytic Association for his assistance, Peter Shankman at HelpAReporter.com without whom this book would have been impossible, and James Strauss, PhD for his continued guidance.

On a personal note, I am so appreciative of my family, Sammy, Chris, Bridgett, Ayesha, Anna, Jannah, Cole, Emma, Madelyn, Maryam; my mother and grandmother, who have always encouraged my scientific pursuits; and my cousins, Rachel, Jeff, Angie and Michael who provide daily encouragement as we travel through life together.

Table of Contents

Author's Introduction

Welcome to the first FAQ of the human brain. I have enlisted the help of experts all over the country to answer your most-secret, most-curious questions, based on their specialties. You can look at the end of each answer to see who answered the question and you can learn more about the contributors by searching the index in the back. I hope this book gives you a greater understanding of yourself, your family and the eccentric woman who lives across the street. Send your own mental health questions to me at Lucy@JLucyBoyd.com for possible inclusion in a future book.

Let the Questions Begin!

What can a person do to help a friend who is having a panic attack?

The best thing you can do to help a friend who has panic attacks is to ask them what they need from you, because the answer is going to vary greatly from person to person. One person might want you to hold their hand and talk, another person might want you to just be silent or even leave the room.

Your friend may or may not be able to tell you want they need while they are in the middle of a panic attack, so it's best to have that conversation at some other time. If you are with someone who starts to have a panic attack and they have not told you want they need, here are some general tips for how you can be helpful:

Be knowledgeable: At the very least, you should know that panic attacks are not medical emergencies. They are an extreme experience of bodily symptoms that lasts for approximately 10-15 minutes. Anxiety is our body's way letting us know that danger is present. Our bodies prepare us to either "fight" or "run away" from danger. During a panic attack, however, the body's preparedness for fight or flight is far greater than the need to actually do so, which leaves a person with little or no explanation about how their body is reacting. Understandably so, this experience can be scary and overwhelming. Once a panic attack begins it cannot be stopped in the middle but must run its course.

It's important to know that one cannot have a continual panic attack that lasts for hours, however, it is possible to experience multiple panic attacks in succession. By knowing this fact, you might be able to help your friend to calm down after one attack and before another one begins. Ask them what might help or make a suggestion in a gentle, non-imposing manner. For example you could ask, "Would you like to take a short walk outside? It might help you to move around a little bit."

Stay Calm. If you get highly anxious yourself, you might communicate to your friend that what they are experiencing is indeed an emergency. It is probably not a good idea to barrage your friend with a lot of questions, which some of us do when we get anxious! Rather, if you are a stable, calming presence, you will be in a position to remind your friend that the panic will pass and that they can get through it. You can tell your friend that you are a safe presence, "I am here, and I will help you in any way I am able."

Reassure and validate your friend's feelings. People are generally very scared and upset by the experience of a panic attack. You want to reassure your friend without dismissing their feelings. Avoid the temptation to say something like, "It's nothing, you will be fine." Instead, try saying something like, "I know you feel really scared right now, but it will be over in 10-15 minutes and you can start to feel better." Or you might say, "Hang on, I know you're overwhelmed, but it will end and be over soon."

Jennifer L. Fee, PsyD

What types of treatment actually help people with panic disorder?

There are a few treatment approaches that can help people overcome panic disorder.

Cognitive Behavioral Therapy (CBT): CBT is very popular and has by far the most research support for its effectiveness for helping people to overcome panic disorder. CBT is a directive and structured approach that addresses panic disorder on several different levels. Specifically, this therapy addresses the connection between our thoughts, feelings, behavior, and physical reactions. Interventions target one of these elements at a time, with the goal of influencing all of them. For example, proper abdominal breathing and relaxation techniques primarily address calming physical reactions. The identification and altering of anxiety-producing thoughts to lower anxiety is another approach. Guided Imagery (where you exposure yourself mentally to a feared situation) aims to eliminate the avoidance that has resulted from the experience of panic attacks. CBT can be described as a collaborative, multifaceted, and comprehensive treatment approach to panic disorder.

Neurofeedback: Otherwise known as "brain biofeedback," neurofeedback helps a person train their brain waves to function differently, or more efficiently. It is non-invasive, easy to participate in, and the potential side effects are very rare and mild. While neurofeedback is not approved by the FDA as a treatment for panic disorder, there is a lot of research and clinical support for its effectiveness. Additionally, there is support that the results are permanent.

Eye Movement Desensitization and Reprocessing (EMDR): EMDR is a treatment approach that was developed for helping people overcome the effects of distressing memories and past trauma in a safe and controlled manner. There is a treatment protocol for using EMDR to treat panic disorder, and there appears to be a lot of anecdotal evidence suggesting that EMDR is helpful for eliminating panic and avoidance. On the flip side, there have only been three controlled, published studies to date examining the use of EMDR for panic disorder, with mixed results.

Medication: Medication does not cure panic disorder, but it can be very helpful to calm anxiety and help people engage in other forms of therapy (with a possible exception of the neurofeedback approach). Both antidepressants (such as Prozac and Zoloft) and anti-anxiety medications (such as Klonopin, Xanax and Ativan) have been commonly prescribed for panic disorder for a long time. In recent years, atypical antipsychotics have also been prescribed to help block panic attacks and lower anxiety.

Many people are afraid to take medication at the prescribed therapeutic dose which therefore limits its ability to be helpful. Since medication is not a cure for anxiety, it's appropriate to use it in conjunction with some other form of treatment. Also, working with a knowledgeable psychiatrist (as opposed to a family doctor) increases one's chances of finding and using medication appropriately.

Jennifer L. Fee, PsyD

My teenager is acting strangely. How do I know if she is on drugs or experiencing a mental problem?

The life of the teenager is filled with hormones, intense interactions and increased responsibilities. This stew makes for strange behavior in previously normal-seeming kids. Some signs of drug or alcohol abuse include:

1. A new group of friends, who are either disrespectful to you, avoid you or seem polite but stay out of your way as much as possible.

2. Watch for the obvious signs of slurred speech, drunken behavior, strange bottles, cigarettes, weird smells, pills, aerosol cans, etc.

3. A sudden loss of interest in school, old friends, family activities or pets.

4. Chronic rule violations such as staying out past curfew and becoming hateful when questioned.

Some signs of mental health problems include:

1. Change in appearance. A girl who wore makeup and nice clothing suddenly doesn't seem to care what her clothing, hair or face looks like.

2. Sleeping too much or too little.

3. A drastic change in eating habits. Watch for your child to lose weight because she isn't eating properly. He may gain weight due to eating for emotional reasons.

4. Stating that he is a loser or that he may as well give up. Loss of interest in extracurricular activities or maintaining grades. Poor self-confidence and negativity concerning the future.

5. Rage out of the bounds of reasonable for the situation. She seems angry most of the time and doesn't want to talk about it.

Lucy

What causes ADHD?

There isn't one cause for ADHD, or attention-deficit hyperactivity disorder. Some cases are felt to be genetic, meaning that an ancestor, usually a parent, also suffers or suffered from the disorder. Theories include environmental toxins, premature birth and problems during pregnancy. The brain chemicals in children with ADHD are different than those of other children, and brain scans show less activity in certain areas of the brain in sufferers. Children shouldn't be scolded or punished for having the disorder; they should be helped to find outlets for their energy and tools to help them focus in the classroom. Some people "outgrow" ADHD but, for others, it continues into adulthood, affecting job performance and relationships. Mental health professionals can help individuals and families cope with the stress of this challenging disorder and recommend medication when necessary.

Lucy

How does a person know whether their sexual interests are normal or pathological?

"Normal" really refers to average behavior. Consequently, what is considered normal in terms of sexuality is simply what most people, or "average" people (whatever that is) think or do in their own sex life. Anything that differs from that could be considered out of the norm. Now, this does not necessarily imply that an interest or behavior is pathological. The term "pathological" refers to a condition that is causing a diseased state. In terms of sexual interests, something would be pathological if it interfered with their ability to function in their life. This could refer to one's ability to socialize appropriately with their peers or maintain a relationship.

Functioning also includes the ability of someone to work and maintain themselves. The classic areas that one looks to in order to evaluate pathology are those of love, work, and play. There are, however, many sexual interests and behaviors that are not considered "normal" but are not necessarily "pathological." Some of these instead might be considered kinky or perverse. Such behaviors exist on a spectrum from a mild interest that is not needed absolutely for sexual gratification, to those interests which are the only method by which a person can achieve sexual gratification. A person may have a certain perversion without it affecting their personal relationships, their work, or their ability to socialize or take care of themselves. For these people, it is simply a matter of finding others with their particular fetish or perversion to share it with. Oftentimes, a person will be part of a larger community that enjoys a particular kink or perversion (think of BDSM or furries).

If a particular sexual interest or behavior does interfere with a person's functioning, or it causes harm to themselves or others, then it may be considered pathological.

Madeleine M. Castellanos, MD

If a person cannot have sex or doesn't have an interest in sex, should they encourage their spouse to find other sex partners for their spouse's mental or physical health?

It is an expectation of marriage that a couple will be having sex and have some natural desire to do so. Regular sexual activity also contributes to greater emotional and physical health. Still, loss of sexual desire to some level affects most couples at one time or another. If a person is in a marriage, one would assume that they did at one time have some interest in sex with their partner. Anytime that a person has had sexual desire and interest in the past, but that has changed over time, I recommend that they explore that with a qualified sex therapist.

There could be a multitude of reasons why a person has lost their interest in sex. These range from the physical (medical illness, hormonal disruptions, medication side effects, poor diet, substance use) to the emotional (depression, anxiety) to relationship issues (anger, fear, resentment, poor communication). I would not recommend bringing other partners into the relationship, or having one partner go outside of the relationship for sex, until these other issues have been addressed. This is because having a sexual relationship outside of the marriage brings a multitude of issues that result in further distancing of the couple, and in many cases, results in the breakup of the couple. Many times, a person may experience a significant decrease in their sexual desire as a result of the natural progression of their relationship. This is often misunderstood as loss of desire for the partner, when in reality it is a change from the lust that results from the great release of dopamine in the beginning of a relationship to the greater stability of conscious love and commitment that develops as the dopamine stops overshadowing the experience.

There are people who never really have any interest in sex. Some of these people may be having difficulty with this because of emotional issues related to experiences earlier in their life. This can also be addressed with a sex therapist in order to explore what may be preventing a person from enjoying their own sexuality. But this is not always the case with those who have never recognized a desire within themselves for sex. Some people are considered to be "asexual" in that they really do not have, and never have had, any real interest or desire in sex. They are perfectly content to live their lives without having sex, ever. If they should enter into a marriage before recognizing this in themselves, or if they thought it would somehow change after marriage, their partners could experience a great deal of frustration. At that time, there should be a very serious discussion of how to proceed in the marriage. There are as many different ways to negotiate a marriage, as there are different personalities in the world. There are people who are able to have an open marriage very successfully, which could be a viable option for such a couple. But not everyone can happily negotiate an open marriage. Remember, the incidence of a person in a marriage having no interest due to asexuality is very small compared to those people who experience a drop off of their sexual desire for other reasons mentioned above.

Madeleine M. Castellanos, MD

Is there really such a thing as "closure" when a loved one dies?

There are many different beliefs on closure, but, in my experience, I've found that closure is more of a concept than a reality. The grief and sense of loss when a loved one dies may diminish in intensity over the years, but there is no point for most people when they decide or realize they are no longer grieving. You may go from thinking of the person many times a day to thinking of them a few times a week or a few times a day, but don't feel that something is wrong if you don't get the closure you hear others talking about. If you remain in so much grief that you cannot function in your everyday life after a year of grieving, however, you should seek grief counseling to help you find peace, and eventually joy, in your life. Seeking out grief counseling does NOT mean you are disrespecting the memory of your loved one or that you are wishing to forget them. Instead, consider it as something to help you survive the grief, as they would wish you to do.

Lucy

Should kids be given responsibilities?

Kids benefit from being given responsibility in several ways.

1. They develop a sense of productivity, pride and accomplishment.

2. They feel a sense of belonging in their family and community.

3. They begin to learn that responsibility and privilege are intertwined.

4. They are prepared for the many responsibilities of adulthood.

Wondering how to introduce responsibility to your child? Here are some tips.

1. Begin teaching responsibility as early as possible and make it fun. Young children love to participate and don't see routine work as boring if the entire family is participating. Allow your child to pick up items from the floor, sort towels, set the dinner table or feed the fish while the rest of the family is doing similar work in the same room. Praise her accomplishments.

2. Keep responsibility simple and as enjoyable as possible. Don't assign your child the work you don't want to do yourself, such as washing the dishes everyday. Instead, keep the tasks pertinent to the child (keep your room neat) or pertinent to her interests (wash the car and you can drive it on Saturday). Remember that assigning responsibility is for her ultimate benefit, not yours.

3. Make sure tasks are age-appropriate. Children under 11 shouldn't have responsibilities that take more than one hour per week, and older children and teens shouldn't have responsibilities that take more than 30 minute per day or a few hours per week.

4. Tie responsibilities to privileges when possible. A child who dusts the family room can choose the family movie, a child who helps with dinner can choose the dinner menu on Tuesday night, and a child who cleans out her closet can have a friend over to spend the night.

5. Saddling children with too much responsibility can backfire. A child who must do much of the family chores may become resentful and decide that she will only work in the future when she is forced to. Ideally, your child will grow up happy to assume her own responsibilities and a small part of the family's responsibilities.

Lucy

Is eating too much considered an addiction?

Historically, medical and professional communities have drawn a strict boundary between substance addictions and other compulsive behaviors. The mindset is held by most of the general public. Most recently, however, the debate has been renewed, with the perspective that compulsive eating, gambling and sex behaviors are also addictions gaining ground.

In the broadest sense, addiction is defined as any behavior that continues despite negative consequences. Think about the potential consequences of compulsive overeating: eating more and more to get the same sense of satisfaction; eating more than intended; excessive weight gain leading to damaged self-esteem; increased risk for cholesterol, diabetes, heart disease, and arthritis, among other physical illnesses; and repeated unsuccessful attempts to control eating. Now, look at the DSM-IV (a book used by mental health professionals) diagnostic criteria for substance dependence, the most severe form of drug addiction. An individual only needs 3 of the following 7 criteria in a one-year period to meet the diagnosis:

1. Tolerance: using increased amount of the substance to get the same effect
2. Withdrawal: substance is taken to relieve characteristic symptoms that develop when the substance is not taken
3. Substance is taken in larger amounts and for longer periods than intended
4. Persistent desire or repeated unsuccessful attempts to quit
5. Much time is spent to obtain, use, or recover from the substance

---

6. Important social, occupational, or recreational activities given up or reduced because of the substance use
7. Use continues despite knowledge of adverse consequences (i.e. emotional, social or physical)

The similarity between symptoms of substance dependence and overeating is not coincidence. Research studies have demonstrated that the appetite for food is housed in the mesolimbic dopamine pathway (also known as the reward pathway) — the same part of the brain that houses the appetite for drugs. Other pathways that are intimately involved in drug addiction including the corticolimbic pathway (important for motivation) and endocannabinoid systems (important in the hunger sensation) are also intimately involved in compulsive overeating.

So, yes, if substance dependence is an addiction, which it is, compulsive overeating can be and should be considered an addiction.

Nzinga Harrison, MD

Is addiction ever strictly a chemical process, i.e., the person can take medication for it and no longer have an addiction, or does it always have emotional and cognitive components?

In short, no. Addiction is never strictly a chemical process that can be cured with a medication. There is always an emotional and cognitive component. Consider the same question for high blood pressure, diabetes, or high cholesterol. When an individual is diagnosed with either of those illnesses, in addition to prescribing a medication, the physician gives education about the causes and management of the illness to address the cognitive components, as well as making recommendations about stress management and dietary change to address the emotional and lifestyle components of the illness.

Addiction is no different. While medications can be very helpful at helping to curb cravings and decrease the risk of relapse to alcohol or drugs, an individual has to recognize the situations or emotions that are likely to cause cravings or increase the risk for relapse—just as an individual with diabetes has to know that eating cheesecake will increase the risk that his blood sugar will be uncontrolled.

The viewpoint that addiction is always a combination of biological, psychological and social factors is not equivalent to the belief that all addictions require a full course of rehabilitation to be controlled. Each medical illness has a spectrum of severity — there are individuals who are diagnosed with diabetes who change their lifestyle with diet and exercise, and completely manage their blood sugar without medication. On the other end of the spectrum, there are individuals diagnosed with diabetes who change their diet, increase their exercise, take insulin and oral diabetic medications, and continue to have uncontrolled blood sugars and repeated hospitalizations despite following all medical recommendations. The illness of addiction is the same. There are some individuals who develop addiction, and with lifestyle changes are able to control their use. Likewise, there are individuals on the other end of the spectrum who attempt to follow all recommendations, and yet, continue to struggle with uncontrolled symptoms of addiction.

In either case, whether addiction or diabetes, an individual has a better chance at achieving remission, or complete control of his symptoms, if the biological, cognitive and emotional aspects of the illness are addressed.

Nzinga Harrison, MD

What is prodromal schizophrenia?

Prodromal is the period in which you are beginning to get sick but don't quite realize it yet. There is evidence that some people enter a prodromal state prior to full-blown schizophrenia and that people with prodromal schizophrenia don't always go on to become schizophrenic. Early detection and mental health care is critical. Prodromal schizophrenia can occur during the first half of life and usually shows up during the teens or twenties. Most people don't realize they are having symptoms, so it is up to family members or close friends to recognize something is wrong. These signs are usually mixed with periods in which the person seems to be their normal self, but possibly quieter or distracted. Signs include:

1. Expression of unusual thoughts. The person may suddenly begin to claim he is a prophet, from another planet, or able to control others with his thoughts. He may seem to be hallucinating (seeing or hearing things you don't see or hear), but this is infrequent at this stage and may go unrecognized by others.

2. Declining interests. The person may quit bathing or brushing his hair and may stop attending social events or showing an interest in much-loved hobbies. He may appear disinterested in the conversations of friends.

3. Suspiciousness. The person may seem to be suspicious of family members or long-time friends. He may suspect that his neighbors are spying on him or that his boss or teacher is out to get him. Alternatively, his suspiciousness may not be voiced, but be recognized by refusing to leave his food in the presence of friends or family members or taking excessive steps to hide his phone calls or everyday plans. He may seem uneasy most of the time.

Lucy

Why is mental health important? Won't it take care of itself?

Your mental health is arguably as important as your physical health, because if it is poor, it can substantially affect your quality of life, ability to have personal relationships and job performance. In some instances, poor mental health can even cause you to kill yourself, purposely, accidentally, or through self-neglect. It can also cause you to wind up in prison. Good mental health contributes to happiness, good decision-making and prosperity. For some people, good mental health seems to come naturally, while others must work to maintain the best mental health they can.

Lucy

Why can't I stop thinking about a woman who doesn't love me?

Obsession is dangerous. It is dangerous for you and it can be dangerous for her if you don't handle it properly. Forget the ideas of romantic love being obsessive; you are dealing with some kind of deficit inside yourself, you might call it a hole, inside you that you think you need her to fill. You may have one of these issues:

1. You may always want what you cannot have. Do you tend to lose interest in a woman once she reciprocates your interest and begins to need things from you? Do you find a thrill in the chase? Do you privately feel that anyone who would like you is not worth much, but someone who ignores you is worth pursuing?

2. If you had a relationship for a period of time, but things have ended, you may be suffering from separation anxiety. This brings a sense of "I can't live without this person." Many men who have this also had issues with their mother leaving as a child, either literally through death or divorce, or figuratively by working outside the home.

3. You may have control issues. It may disturb you that she is going through life without needing you. It may bother you that she is dating someone else. These control issues often lead to anger management problems and it is imperative that you get ahold of them with counseling. Don't, I repeat don't, do something foolish and turn a short-term problem into a long-term one. Tell yourself, the situation just isn't worth it and fill your mind with projects worthy of your attention.

4. You may be having a severe grief response. This is often the case when a long-term relationship ends. The severity is often dictated by other perceived losses in your life, whether time with your children, your lifestyle as you knew it, your future dreams, etc. You may have a foreboding feeling that "this can't end well" or be experiencing depression. Seek counseling to help you deal with this unresolved grief. You deserve to be happy and only by getting past this in a healthy way will you find it.

Lucy

If a child wishes to participate in a team sport, but decides he doesn't like it after the uniform, helmet, etc., is purchased and the season is underway, what should the parent do?

1.   Is the child having fun? Can fun be infused into the sport more? Research has shown that the number one reason both boys and girls stop participating in organized sports is because it's no longer fun. This typically happens around late pre-adolescence, age 11 to 12 or so.

2.   Before even starting, thoroughly explain the team/sport/time requirement so the child will have some sort of expectation. Keep in mind, kids explore multiple interests. Parents should guide them in not being over-extended.

3.   Consider the child's developmental level regarding time, abstract thinking, and social skills. Is the activity slow? Is there enough physical engagement like running?

4.   Is the child over-extended and simply exhausted with too many activities?

5.   Is something happening in the activity that the child is avoiding? Things to consider could be embarrassment, bullying, lacking talent or skill, or lacking social skill.

6.   Has the child observed a parent withdrawing from adult activities or responsibilities? Has this "quitting" behavior been modeled for the child or in some way condoned by parents in the past?

7.   Once parents have determined that no negative factors above are contributing to onset of disinterest, it's important to share family values with the child about commitment to people who are counting on them, commitment to finishing something that others are also working on, commitment to priorities, etc.

8.   For younger kids, an additional incentive may be helpful for them to stay engaged in the sport. For example, a favorite snack or a movie after games/practice, etc. Keep in mind, you're trying to reinforce tenacity and commitment and you're not bribing your kid to continue.

9.   If it simply seems unbearable for the child to continue in the sport, have them trade for another activity, not just completely quitting. Help them find other things that are important to them.

10. Sport will always be one of the best metaphors for life. The child, even when deciding to terminate his or her participation, is still being exposed to a life lesson that will certainly and eventually resurface.

Jeffrey L. Brown, PsyD

What qualities can I instill in my child to help him be successful as an adult?

There are many qualities that can be taught to children that are also helpful in reaching success as an adult. Clearly, bad qualities can be taught as well. Therefore, parents, grandparents and other caregivers must be deliberate and intentional about the values they teach and the character they try to develop in kids.

While the list of critical developmental tasks for children has almost an infinite number of items on it, a few key considerations should rise to the surface. First, teaching kids a healthy self-concept--what a kid believes is his or her own personal definition as a person--is critical. Many kids who are taught to think positively and accurately about their own abilities, worth, likeability, social prowess and competence have an adult to thank. Research is clear that kids need a stable, consistent adult in their lives to help manage stress and use as a model for living life. As adults, the tasks are easier than we might think. Spend time with kids, verbally praise them, give them responsibilities that can lead them to success. Be cautious that you don't send the wrong message to a kid. For example, if you never spend time with your child, the child may believe that he or she has no value and that other things in your life are more important. They can begin to believe wrongly about their own value and hence try to find that value in other, often negative, domains of life--poor relationships, acting out behaviors, etc.

Along with a positive self-identity will almost naturally come resilience. As parents we can foster resilience by teaching kids how to think about accepting failure well. Failure is a routine part of life and learning to negotiate it, rather than fear it, is an important task for kids to learn. All too often, kids are rescued by parents who also can't stand it if they see kids fail. Parents fail too and having a joint partnership with your kid around how you and/or your family deal with failure is a good idea. Parents first must look at how they themselves deal with failure, then decide what messages they are sending to their kids, either directly or indirectly. Does your child see you bounce back, try again, or otherwise calibrate skills to get a job done well? They should be seeing that and hearing you describe why you're doing what you're doing. Dealing well with failure is an important part of success. Offering your child novel experiences is also one way of helping them navigate the future. Letting them safely learn through trial and error--or simply exploring something new--helps them build the parts of their brain that will allow them to navigate similar situations in the future.

Lastly, give your kids opportunities to be socially successful. In our current internet age, it's too easy to let kids have virtual relationships on social networking sites, through email or on video games. Kids need face to face time with peers — they need to build a history with people and learn to interact successfully. Parents should make sure they are doing the same, again, modeling social success for your child.

Jeffrey L. Brown, PsyD

How can I guard my mental health?

1. Recognize problems such as depression, anxiety, addiction and obsessive thinking, and seek treatment.

2. Keep a balance of productivity and free time in your life. If you don't have a career, find other ways to make a difference in society, by creating art, volunteering, helping the earth, mentoring a child or being kind to an animal. There are many ways to contribute. Just make sure you keep enough of your time for yourself by refusing to overextend yourself with responsibilities. A typical workweek is 40 hours long and you shouldn't allow yourself to work more than that on a regular basis. Avoid having more children that you can reasonably provide care to and don't volunteer for extra work if you lack the time and emotional energy to perform the tasks. You should have a couple of free hours each day, at minimum, and one to two days per week in which you can do anything you wish, or nothing at all.

3. Learn effective stress management techniques that work FOR YOU. One person relaxes while fishing, another feels calm while jogging, and still another escapes into a warm bubble bath. Yoga, meditation, spiritual practices, reading, hiking in nature, journaling, watching a funny movie or playing with an animal are all ways that people relieve stress.

4. Avoid toxic relationships and situations. We are greatly affected by our environments and the people around us. Refuse to live with people who aren't loving and supportive; refuse to work with people who belittle or bully you; and get yourself permanently out of on-again, off-again, high-drama relationships, whether they are with lovers, friends or relatives. Just say no to drama. Avoid working or spending time in negative environments, where people, animals or the environment are hurt on a regular basis.

Lucy

My daughter is about to begin dating. What should I tell her?

First, I would tell her that she can always call you to come and get her from any situation without severe consequences. You don't want your daughter to make a bad decision to go to a party that turns frightening and feel forced to stay because she doesn't want to face you. You also don't want her riding home with someone who is drunk or high.

Second, I would tell her that she must never allow herself to be disrespected or abused. I would teach her the signs of relationship abuse, such as threats, coercive behavior, controlling behavior, violence of any kind or blackmailing. She should understand that jealous behavior does not equal love and that people who have jealous tendencies should be avoided.

Third, I would explain to her that she must never send inappropriate pictures of herself to anyone--period--nor should she allow anyone to take a compromising photo of her. I would explain the ways that these photos can be illegal, but, worse, they can ruin her life for many decades to come.

Finally, I would explain what healthy dating feels like. I would teach her the differences between attraction and love and how to respect herself while dating.

Lucy

What is behavioral management?

Behavioral management is a type of therapy that treats
dysfunctional or self-harming behavior. With this type of
therapy, the therapist focuses on getting the client to change
her behavior, rather than spending a lot of time figuring out
what is causing the behavior. I call it the "just stop it"
approach. It does work in some cases, and seems to have
reasonable effectiveness in treating substance abuse disorders
and helping people conquer fears, such as in OCD. I
personally feel it is not the best course of therapy for treating
many serious problems, the kinds that develop as a result of
childhood abuse or other harmful childhood experiences. To
me, these are best treated with psychoanalysis or
psychotherapy, which allows the person to talk about the
experiences and come to terms with them.

Lucy

What is it like to be in a psychiatric hospital?

Short-term psychiatric hospitals will remind you of traditional hospitals in some senses. The staff might wear uniforms, but they are often dressed in street clothes, and your meals are provided in a group setting. You may have a private room or have one roommate. Your vitals signs may be checked every shift, daily or weekly and a nurse will dispense medication for your mental health as well as any medical problems you have. The schedule is often rigid and filled with activities. A typical day may go like this:

7:00 Breakfast
8:00 Morning group session
9:00 Exercise
9:30 Individual therapy
12:00 Lunch
1:00 Vital signs
2:00 Recreation
3:00 Afternoon group session
4:30 Music and art
5:30 Dinner
7:00 Evening group session
8:00 Movie
10:00 Bedtime

Your visits and phone calls may be restricted and monitored by staff. Depending on your personality, you may accept the rigid structure or you may feel stifled by it. Many facilities use a form of therapy called the therapeutic milieu. This means, simply, that the staff and clients are all working together for a goal, which is improved mental health. While the staff is in charge, they strive to avoid seeming dictatorial in a milieu and may eat and freely converse with the clients. As you might expect, there are lots of group and individual counseling sessions designed to help you look at your problems differently and learn new coping skills.

Long-term psychiatric facilities may have more of the feel of a nursing home than a hospital. Therapy may be given once a week, once a day or more frequently, depending on diagnosis and prognosis. A nurse dispenses medication and mental health technicians assist the clients with daily hygiene activities as needed. Recreational activities are provided and meals are eaten in a group setting when possible. The staff may wear traditional nursing attire. Visitors may be limited.

Lucy

Are there any predators so mentally ill that they are beyond treatment?

As a psychiatrist who has treated many different types of predators, from bad girls and bad boys who break their partner's heart, to actual criminals, I can tell you that no one is beyond treatment. But predators, like others with psychological problems, need the right kind of treatment - intensive psychotherapy. Some predators may need medication as well.

Carole Lieberman, MD

Do recurrent dreams reveal our unconscious desires?

Sigmund Freud said, "Dreams are the royal road to the unconscious." Recurrent dreams are trying to tell us something. They keep recurring in order to get us to pay attention to their symbolic message.

Carole Lieberman, MD

What is dependent personality disorder?

Dependent personality disorder is a type of personality disorder in which the person feels that someone else must take care of them. Ironically, they often achieve this by becoming a caretaker, such as a wife who takes care of her husband but doesn't realize she is being so diligent because she is terrified of being on her own. One obvious downside to this condition is that it leaves the sufferer open to abuse, and many of those with dependent personality disorder do wind up in abusive relationships. It doesn't feel good to be in a relationship with someone who has this disorder because the partner often feels smothered by the sufferer's insecurities. Both parties can benefit from counseling, and, while the changed dynamic may take some adaptation, a chance for a healthy, functional relationship is possible. Single adults with dependent personality disorder may become too intense in new relationships and feel scared or alone when living by themselves. Counseling is beneficial as well as learning to enjoy being with oneself and having the freedom that all adults should cherish.

Lucy

What should I say to a friend whose baby died during pregnancy?

When a baby dies during pregnancy, people are shocked. This is not what is supposed to happen. Despite the rather high rate of miscarriage, few expect this to happen to them, particularly during their first pregnancy, and a stillbirth after the 20th week of pregnancy comes as even more of a shock. Witnessing the grief and sadness that a pregnancy loss causes in the bereaved parents can result in great discomfort in others for many reasons. First of all, when we observe bad things happening to others, it can create a sense that this could happen to us, i.e., a sense of vulnerability. We may feel grateful that it did not happen to us, and then feel ashamed of this feeling and experience survivor guilt as a result. In addition, we can feel helpless in the face of another's crisis, unable to make it better and unable to take away their pain, pain that may last many months, even a year, especially for the bereaved woman. We may also feel awkward, not knowing what to say or do, fearing that whatever we do might make them cry. Our discomfort can result in either our withdrawing from the grieving individual or blurting out some well-intentioned but thoughtless comment that is received as insensitive or dismissive (e.g., "everything happens for a reason," "it happened so early, it wasn't even a baby, yet," or "you can always have another baby").

Rather than withdrawing from the grieving parent or saying something that does not recognize their feelings of loss, here are several suggestions of what you may be able to say or do that can be more helpful to the parents:

48

Just say, "I'm so sorry. I know how much you wanted that baby." This acknowledges the parents' sorrow, their desire for their baby, and their right to grieve.

Ask them if they would like to talk about their loss. If they named their baby and you are aware of this name, use it. This gives them an opening to speak, acknowledges the existence of a real baby to them, yet also respects their need to talk if and when they feel ready.

If the grieving parent does begin to cry in response, let them know it's okay to cry. This validates their feelings and their need to release these feelings without embarrassment in your presence.

Let them know how much you care about them and that you want to help in any way they need. Making specific suggestions of practical help you can offer (e.g., notifying family or friends of their loss; bringing a meal for them, doing their laundry or going for a walk together) may be preferable to asking vaguely if there is anything you can do, as grieving parents may be so overwhelmed they either cannot think of what they need at this time or feel awkward asking you to do anything for them.

Ask if you may call them in a few days to see how they are doing. As time passes, support often disappears for the grieving parents. Those who continue to reach out to them and are available to listen are rare and so meaningful to most grieving individuals, and this continued availability validates for them that you support them in taking the time that they need to heal from this loss.

If you are pregnant or have children yourself, be sensitive to their loss during your own joyful events. For example, try not to drone on about how wonderful your child is nor complain about how difficult the kids are or about your aches and pains of pregnancy. If announcing a pregnancy, don't spring it on the grieving individual in a group setting, and acknowledge when you do share this news with them that you realize this may be difficult for them to hear now. If planning an event such as a bris or baptism, call or write to your friend ahead of time, explaining that you do not want to exclude them as they are important to you and you want them to do what is most comfortable for them. Let them know that you will completely understand whatever they need to do and mean it.

Finally, be patient, as grief can last a long time.

Joann Paley Galst, PhD

Is it true that people are more likely to conceive once they quit dwelling on it, and, if so, what is the reason for it?

Oh, that it were so easy! This is one of the myths that is so hurtful to those struggling with infertility, implying that not obsessing about getting pregnant or "just" relaxing will increase one's chances of pregnancy. If that were the case, everyone would be able to get pregnant in the first three to six months of trying, before they begin getting anxious and/or stressed about it. While there has been much debate on the impact of stress on fertility, there is no unequivocal evidence that stress causes infertility. It is unquestionable, however, that infertility causes stress and frequently causes strain on any relationship. What is so easy for others is so difficult for those struggling with infertility, making the primal urge to procreate difficult for approximately one in six couples.

Another fertility myth is that once you adopt a child you will get pregnant. Although it is not unheard of for a woman to become pregnant after adopting, the statistics do not demonstrate any improvement in fertility as a result of adopting, as the percentage of women getting pregnant after adopting is about 5%, the same as for infertile women who do not adopt. It is also offensive to suggest that adopting a child is only a means to an end rather than a joyous and successful endeavor in and of itself.

Infertility is a disease or condition of the reproductive system affecting approximately 15% of the population, with ~40% due to female and 40% due to male factors, 10% due to a combination of both male and female factors, and ~ 10% unexplained. While relaxing or becoming less "obsessed" with becoming pregnant can improve your overall quality of life, your intense focus and the stress and sadness you feel are the result of infertility, not the cause of it.

If you, as a woman, are under age 35 and have been having unprotected sex for a year (six months if you are 35 or over) and have been unable to conceive, consult a reproductive endocrinologist to determine your fertility treatment options. Once you do that, it may be even harder to focus on anything beyond your fertility, because diagnosis requires a woman to track her menstrual cycle carefully and, if undergoing treatment, that she be acutely aware of cycle days and symptoms to facilitate her following the recommended treatment. Learning relaxation and mindfulness techniques, however, may help you to build your resilience so you are better able to cope with the demands of your treatment (see Stressed for Success: When Infertility Makes you Anxious, Tense, and Ticked Off, published by the American Fertility Association, www.theafa.org/article/stressed-for-success/)

Joann Paley Galst, PhD

What is the best way to discipline a child?

First, babies under two should never be subject to discipline, because they don't have the capacity to understand it nor the ability to consistently control many of their actions. The best discipline is positive discipline, such as getting a reward for helpful behavior or for managing to break a bad habit. Rewards can include increased privileges but shouldn't feel like a bribe. Nor should a reward be something the child has a right to anyway, such as time with a parent. Short timeouts are sometimes effective for young children, provided they aren't presented in a fear-inducing or humiliating way. Instead, a time-out should be presented as a time to cool off and gather oneself emotionally. Yelling, threatening and hitting a child should absolutely be avoided. It is impossible to truly respect someone that you fear, and, in my view, it is impossible to purely love someone you fear as well. To build a healthy life-long relationship with your child, avoid doing things you will regret when they are 30 and you want to spend time with them. Spanking and hitting only teach that the bigger person wins the disagreement—a horrible lesson at any age. Everyone has a right to wake up each morning and know that no one is going to hit them that day. Allow your child her personal space by not violating her body with violence, and she will be less apt to allow others to abuse her in the future.

Children of all ages learn from natural consequences. If they throw a cookie, they don't get another cookie that day. If they tell a lie, they don't have the trust of their parent for a few weeks. Make sure that you know what to expect developmentally. So many parents seem to think that a toddler should have emotional control, and that is just not possible. Tantrums are a part of learning how to control your emotions and they are a natural part of toddlerhood. Put yourself in your child's shoes. Would you want to be taken through store after store and be bored to death, but not be allowed to have any of the things you see? It's unrealistic to expect it of a child, who is often tired, hungry or bored. Never criticize a child for crying as it is a natural response to the intense feelings he has, whether sad, angry, humiliated or frightened. A nurturing parent learns how to anticipate her child's needs and feelings and is prepared to help him cope with them by providing tools such as talking and blowing off steam by playing.

For very young children, it's best to keep trouble from them by monitoring their movements closely. Put away dangerous items, give them age-appropriate toys and feeding utensils and allow them free range to play as much as possible. Stay engaged with them constantly so that you don't wake up one day and realize you don't have a good relationship with your child.

Lucy

What can I do to get in a better mood?

Moods reveal our feelings and our emotional responses to what is going on around us. Try to determine the cause of your bad mood and whether it can be resolved. If this doesn't work, try one of the following:

1. Get busy. Complete a project you've been needing to, one that will give you a sense of accomplishment.

2. Get a good workout. Take a brisk walk or jog, do calisthenics, shoot some basketball hoops or play tennis with a friend.

3. Listen to music that makes you feel good. Current rock and music from my teenage years works for me. If you don't know what to listen to, try club tunes or old-time disco.

4. Write your feelings down and then write out your future goals. Alternatively, write down five things you're grateful for.

5. Watch a funny movie.

6. Get a massage.

7. Play with a dog or pet a cat who will sit with you.

8. Help somebody.

9. Talk to a friend about what's bothering you.

10. Smile! It often improves your mood instantly.

Lucy

Why do people seek out intimate relationships even though they are complicated and frequently don't end well?

Researchers define intimate relationships as trusting and committed relationships between partners that care for and rely on each other (Mashek & Aron, 2004). Intimate relationships are important experiences. As Hal Kelley (1979) stated in his seminal work, *Personal Relationships*, "...in its various manifestations in dating, marriage, cohabitation, and romantic liaisons, the heterosexual dyad is probably the single most important type of personal relationship in the life of the individual and in the history of society. It occasions the greatest satisfactions of life and also the greatest disappointments" (pg. 2).

There are many reasons why individuals pursue intimate relationships. In an evolutionary context, relationships are a crucial element of the human experience and human survival (Buss & Kenrick, 1988). The desire for relationships is so central that some have suggested that humans have a fundamental need to belong that individuals fulfill by forming deep, meaningful relationships with close others (Baumeister & Leary, 1995). Individuals have such a strong need for relationships that individuals in low quality relationships report greater well-being that those who are not dating at all (Dush & Amato, 2005).

Clearly, relationships have their benefits. A primary benefit of intimate relationships is that they typically coincide with the experience of passionate love which is characterized by positive feelings such as arousal and excitement (Berscheid & Walster, 1974). Relationship partners can also help deal with difficult experiences by providing a soothing presence. For example, a study examined brain activation in married women during a task where they anticipated receiving a shock (Coan, Schaefer, & Davidson, 2006). When women held their husband's hand rather than a male stranger's hand or no hand at all, their brain registered the shock as less threatening; the benefit of holding the husband's hand was greater if the couple has better relationship quality.

Of course, divorce is common and non-marital break-up even more so (Lewandowski & Radice, in press). Making the transition from marriage to divorce is one of the most significant life stressors that an individual can experience (Holmes & Rahe, 1967). Often when relationships end, individuals experience feelings of depression and anxiety (Boelen & Reijntjes, 2009). However, when a relationship ends that did not provide the individual with opportunities for self growth, those individuals experience more positive emotions and positive changes to the self-concept (Lewandowski & Bizzoco, 2007).

Gary W. Lewandowski, Jr., PhD

Is chronic pain often due to psychological reasons? Does it mean the person is a hypochondriac?

Thanks to brain scans such as the functional MRI, scientists are discovering that physical pain and psychological pain aren't as different as we have thought. Psychological pain can cause us to feel physical pain more strongly and physical pain can leave us emotionally weak and vulnerable. For some people, emotional pain can be expressed as a backache, fear may be felt as a stomachache, and stress can be felt as a headache. This does not mean the person is a hypochondriac.

Treatment needs to focus on both the physical and psychological pain; a pain management physician and a mental health professional working in tandem can help in these cases. Empathy from family members and friends is sometimes helpful but allowing the person's chronic pain to dictate the family schedule can lead to unhealthy patterns. For these reasons, it is beneficial to bring in a mental health professional who can facilitate healing and healthy family dynamics.

Lucy

What is the best treatment for schizophrenia, medication or psychotherapy?

If one were to use only one modality, it would be pharmacotherapy. With the exception of a very small number of studies, which have no statistical validity, the overwhelming study consensus is that pharmacotherapy is essential for the treatment of schizophrenia-you might say a sine qua non, or necessary part. Studies, as well as the experience of most practitioners, is that a combination of these treatments produce the best results as to the illness itself and the quality of life the individual is to have. The compliance with medications also greatly improves through the psychotherapy alliance. There is much to say about this subject but the bottom line is that schizophrenia treatment without neuroleptics is not feasible .

Samuel Mowerman, MD

What is situational depression?

Situational depression involves a premise that some, if not most, mental health professionals follow. It looks at whether someone is depressed due to a situation, rather than due to a chemical change in the brain. For example, if someone loses a child and their spouse is slowly dying of cancer, many people might think, "I would be depressed, too!" Other situations that can induce depression include being in an unhappy marriage, suffering from chronic physical pain, chronic worry due to employment loss, etc. In many of these situations, it is better to try to improve the circumstances rather than merely prescribe an antidepressant. Depression is often a clue that someone feels a sense that they aren't in control of their life. It is common in abused women, for example. But rather than simply treat the depression, it is better to leave the abusive situation and the depression may ease on its own. Some cases of depression are felt to be chemical, meaning that nothing appears to be wrong in the person's life, yet they feel depressed. These ideas become quite complex and it is often hard to figure out which comes first. When someone has full-blown depression, both medication and psychotherapy may be needed. As the person begins to feel better, he may desire to look at making changes in his life to reduce the possibility of becoming depressed in the future. He may also develop new friendships, exercise routines, coping mechanisms and interests that can lower the risk of future depression.

Lucy

Is it a good idea to homeschool a child with an anxiety disorder?

Most children benefit from the socialization found at school. They learn how to get along with peers and deal with authority figures, skills that they will use later in the job market. They develop friendships and learn the ups and downs of many types of relationships. As far as learning, it can be done in the classroom, at home or via the internet. Going to school is really for the socialization more so than the learning these days, given that the learning can take place in many ways.

A child with an anxiety disorder may be helped by spending time with her peers. Friends can be of comfort and the actual process of being around others on a daily basis may serve as a type of therapy in itself, similar to the exposure therapy sometimes utilized to treat anxiety disorders. Children with severe anxiety, panic attacks and severe social anxiety disorder may need "breaks" from school during which time they are homeschooled, tutored or taught via the internet. A therapist should be a part of any decision such as this, as taking a child out of school may reinforce the notion that it isn't safe to be around others, doing more harm than good for some children.

Lucy

Do you feel that most people with developmental disabilities have a good quality of life? Many people considering abortion of a fetus with a developmental disability wonder about this.

When we talk about developmental disabilities we are really talking about a very wide range of disorders that differ greatly in terms of physical, cognitive, and adaptive presentation. It includes mental retardation, cerebral palsy, epilepsy, neurological impairment, dyslexia, autism spectrum disorders, and other genetic disorders that are associated with impaired adaptive and cognitive functioning. For example, Down's Syndrome is the most common of the genetic disorders affecting one in 800 to 1,000 births. Most are mildly to moderately cognitively affected and can live relatively independent lives, while some will require adult supervision at all times for the rest of their lives. Key features of Down's Syndrome are mental retardation and extensive medical problems such as thyroid dysfunction, congenital heart defects, and obstructive sleep apnea. Autism is another developmental disability that has a wide range of functioning levels varying from those with profound mental retardation to Asperger's Syndrome that is marked by average or higher intellectual capability but poor socialization and odd behaviors. These individuals can achieve success and a relatively high quality of life.

There are other, less common, genetic disorders, including Fragile X (1 in 3,600 males and 1 in 4000 to 6000 females) in which 50-60 percent have autism. Prader Willi is rare (1 in 10,000 – 15,000) and is associated with morbid obesity, aggression and skin picking. Smith-Magenis is even more rare (1 in 25,000) and is associated with self-injurious behaviors, scoliosis, frequent tantrums, aggression, autistic features, and sleep problems. Cornelia de Lange (1 in 10,000 to 30,000) is also associated with self-injurious behaviors and aggression toward others. Lesch-Nyhan (1 in 380,000 births) is, again, associated with severe self-injurious behaviors including biting of the lips and tongue and, as the person gets older, biting of the feet and fingers, head banging, and scratching. In most cases, the more severe the genetic disorder, the less likely that the pregnancy will reach full term as severe chromosomal problems result in miscarriage.

As far as the consideration of abortion, parents will be more concerned with the developmental disabilities that have a genetic component as described above, as those are the ones that will become evident through the more invasive testing available during pregnancy. The quality of life for an individual with a developmental disability, taken broadly, is very difficult to qualify as it depends on the specific disorder and the degree of impairment the afflicted person will suffer as the disorder presents itself differently among individuals. There are many interventions available now that target specific deficits in functioning beginning in very early childhood. Generally, I have found that the intellectual functioning is the key indicator of the quality of life for the individual. Those with mild to moderate cognitive delays can live more independent to semi-independent productive lives, while those with severe to profound cognitive delays will require much support. [Statistics from National Down Syndrome Society and US National Library of Medicine's Genetics Home Reference]

Mentwab Wuhib, PhD

How do you know if you're psychotic?

Psychosis is marked by delusions, hallucinations, disorganized speech or thought, and disorganized or catatonic behavior. The types of psychotic disorders include schizophrenia, schizophreniform disorder, schizoaffective disorder, delusional disorder, brief psychotic disorder, and shared psychotic disorder.

Whether individuals are aware that they have a psychotic disorder to begin with (not whether they are experiencing it at the time) depends on the severity of the psychosis. From my work with adults with severe and chronic mental illness marked with psychosis, many displayed poor judgment and lacked insight into their illness. The more disabled they were from the illness, the less insight they had into their psychosis. To them, the delusions and hallucinations were real and the work becomes about teaching them how to manage and live alongside the symptoms where medications do not fully address the symptoms as was often the case. Individuals who fully remit after psychotic episodes or are mildly affected may be able to *retrospectively* realize that their behaviors were out of touch with reality and can benefit from psychoeducation that focuses on teaching them more about their illness and its presentation and ways to identify reality from fantasy as well as implement coping mechanisms to manage the symptoms. Hence, it is one thing to *know* that one has a psychotic disorder following the labeling that has been given by mental health professionals, but another to know that one is actually experiencing psychosis at the time that it's occurring.

By definition, individuals in a psychotic episode have lost touch with reality and their world is the real world. They are not aware that they are in a psychotic episode: By definition, a delusion is a *false belief* that is firmly held despite what everyone else believes or the existence of evidence to the contrary. Those affected may know that something is wrong but not that they have psychosis per se or that they are having an episode at the time it's occurring. In response to the individual's statement, "What if I'm insane and I don't know it," the indicator is the impact that his or her behavior has upon their overall functioning and on others, e.g., family, relationships, work, school. There is a lot of feedback that their environment provides them to give them clues that something is wrong. I would want to know, first, why this person is asking such a question as there are many reasons that individuals have a fear of becoming "insane," e.g., this is associated with panic disorder and significant anxiety. It may not be "insanity" that they are really afraid of, but of losing control, which can be still a very frightening but normal response to many situations.

Mentwab Wuhib, PhD

Should all children be given a sports trophy, regardless of whether they were victorious?

While all children should be praised for effort and participation, trophies or high praise given regardless of results can lead to a loss of the sense of healthy pride in one's accomplishments in life, a strong motivator for positive behavior. Children should be encouraged to find ways in which they excel, whether in sports, academics or helping others, and one area shouldn't be stressed as more important than the others. For example, the child who excels in chess should be praised just as much as the one who helps the team win the football championship. Likewise, the child who volunteers to work at the local pet shelter should be given positive attention by parents and grandparents.

Lucy

How many couples decide not to marry after having premarital counseling and what are the typical causes underlying the decision?

It's really hard to give a definitive number. Probably most continue to proceed with their plans because for many, the decision to marry is an emotional one and not necessarily a clearly thought out one. It's unromantic to consider that a relationship is work and that the glow of attraction and emotion will fade as the marriage continues. At this point in their relationship, couples often think that they are immune to problems. However, some couples — especially those who are experiencing a great sense of disrespect for one another realize that this is likely to continue and will be courageous enough to call off the plans.

Some couple also go ahead with plans because there has already been such an investment set in motion…a venue has been chosen, music has been arranged, flowers have been ordered, etc. Emotionally, there may be a sense that parents will be let down.

Of course, the best scenario is the one where couples enter premarital counseling because they recognize that in order to have a solid relationship they need to have the proper expectations about what marriage means. They are willing to learn what it takes to have a partnership and be there for one another in a caring, loving way. With this mindset and openness, this couple will have a road map that will help to guide them as they go forward.

Karen Sherman, PhD

Should couples experiencing empty nest syndrome focus on spending more time together or on developing their own interests?

In order to deal with the empty nest syndrome, couples should really start preparing many years before it is actually going to occur. The couple should start to talk about how they envision this time of life. What do they hope to do, what are their fears, what are their dreams?

Surprisingly, part of that preparation should be making sure that the children are, in fact, independent and capable of taking care of themselves. If they are not, then the parents won't really be able to enjoy this new phase of life. As far as whether the couple should spend time together or as individuals, probably it should be a combination of both and will depend on the individuals. This is a time that affords them an opportunity to do things that there hasn't been time to do, a time to try things that they may have always had an interest in but never felt entitled to, and an opportunity to learn new things together or apart.

Karen Sherman, PhD

Do you think most parents would benefit from a child development class, or is parenting instinctual?

Child development classes are helpful for all parents and soon-to-be parents. While some parts of parenting are instinctual, such as protecting and feeding the child, it is critical to understand the social, mental, physical, emotional and behavioral developmental stages of the child so that expectations are appropriate. Too many parents expect small children to be able to sit still through a movie, dinner, store visit or doctor appointment and this isn't realistic. Similarly, they expect children to be able to easily accept disappointment, when this often isn't possible. Many parents don't understand that children cry from frustration, fear and embarrassment, not merely to manipulate their parents or get their own way. Parents should also understand that ten minutes to an adult may feel like an hour to a child. Being on queue regarding a child's ability helps parents nurture their child and explore each day with loving eyes rather than annoyance.

Lucy

Are we less able to cope with stress than our ancestors, and, if so, why? Our ancestors coped with having large numbers of children, horrible diseases that wiped out both children and adults, and family separations without the ability to readily communicate. It seems that we have it relatively easy compared to them.

Those who live in the industrialized countries of today (i.e., the United States, Europe and Asia) have it enormously easier than our ancestors did in terms of how demanding and stressful life is. This is true for one major reason: the more you go back in time, the less scientific and technological advancement there was.

Before the industrial revolution of the eighteenth and nineteenth centuries, life was extremely brutal and short. Many people don't realize how hard life was before the invention of all of our modern conveniences. There was no modern plumbing, hot water, electricity, air conditioning, heating, computers, cars, cell phones, airplanes, modern medicine, grocery stores, and a million other products and services that make our lives so much more comfortable and easier than our ancestors'. Life before all of these wonderful conveniences was filled with drudgery, famine, pestilence, and filth, with an average life expectancy of about 40 or less-- half of the current average life expectancy of nearly 80 in the industrialized world.

It was certainly more stressful to have to hunt for your breakfast in the wilderness with a spear than driving in a heated Toyota to Starbuck's. In order for people to survive in the past, they had to be more resilient and rugged, otherwise they would quickly die (which many did).

However, how stressful something is and how well one copes with that stress are two separate issues. It doesn't necessarily follow that the more stress someone is under, the better coping skills they will possess. The reason for this is that the ability to cope with stress is based on the internal abilities of a person, not on the external demands of the period the person lives in.

So, are we less able to cope than our ancestors? This is an extremely difficult question to answer for several reasons. To begin with, we have no reliable way of assessing how well people of today cope with stress compared to their ancestors. The main reason is that there is no data to compare the coping abilities of someone living today with someone living a hundred or more years ago. Currently, we have ways of assessing people's coping ability, and have instruments that measure stress levels. However, we didn't have these measures a hundred or more years ago; thus, all we can do is speculate about the coping abilities of different generations of people.

Another difficulty in answering this question is that the ability to cope with stress is individual, so you can't really make a blanket statement about how well whole generations of people comparably cope or coped with stress. Whether past or present, some people cope very well with stress and others don't. This is because some people have acquired particular skills that allow them to manage and minimize stress, while others haven't learned these skills or were never motivated enough to learn them. This is true whether you are living today or five hundred years ago. Some examples of coping skills of today would be time management skills, organization skills, communication and assertiveness skills, and many more. Several hundred years ago, different coping skills might have been more important, such as being able to cope with a significantly more precarious and physically demanding lifestyle (although this is also true for most people today in the non-industrialized countries).

In addition, another element that makes comparing coping abilities between generations challenging is that the external conditions of life are so different now as compared with our ancestors. It's like comparing apples and oranges. Life for our ancestors was significantly more stressful because of the excruciating physical realities of life back then. The further you go back in time, the more physically demanding, and inherently stressful, life was.

But, even though life was much more stressful for our ancestors, it is impossible to assess whether they coped better with their brutal living conditions than we currently cope with our significantly less stressful lives, because the skills required to cope with stress in each generation are so different.

So who coped or copes better—our ancestors or us? Did the caveman who was able to kill large prey, sleep on a rock, make his own tools, and survive to age 26 cope better than a modern woman who is able to successfully raise three kids, manage a full-time career, survive breast cancer, and live to age 80? How do you compare the two?

What one can definitely say is that people living in today's modern, industrialized societies have a much better chance of survival and enjoyment of life than our ancestors did, even with less ability to cope. Why? Because we have amazing products and services that make coping much easier. When we're hot, we can turn on the air conditioning. When we're hungry, we can drive to the nearest convenience store. When we're sick, we can get a shot and be treated with the most advanced modern medicine. Even if you are poor today in an industrialized society, you live better than royalty did a few hundred years ago.

I think the most important idea to take from this is that whatever age you live in, to survive and thrive in life, it is vital to learn and utilize the specific coping skills that will allow you to successfully manage whatever life throws at you, whether a saber-toothed tiger or a traffic jam on your work commute.

Steve Orma, PsyD

What are some effective stress management tools for men who think yoga, meditation, or a hot bath isn't for them?

The key point to keep in mind when choosing activities to manage stress is to find ones that reflect your personal tastes, interests, and values. They should also be relaxing, fun, and comfortable to you personally. If the activity doesn't provide these, it isn't going to relieve stress, no matter how many other people find it useful.

For many women and men, yoga, meditation, and a hot bath are enjoyable and de-stressing activities. However, some men (and some women) may not favor them. For some men, these activities may seem "too feminine" and therefore, they feel uncomfortable or self-conscious engaging in them. Or, it just may be that it's not their thing. This is completely okay, as there are an unlimited variety of hobbies and activities that men and women can engage in that provide the same benefits as yoga, meditation, and hot baths.

Here are some suggestions:

Exercise — This can include any type of aerobic exercise (e.g., swimming, running, hiking, cycling, skiing, walking) or strength-based exercise (e.g., weight lifting, machines, push-ups, crunches, pull-ups).
Sports — Playing a sport can be a fun and sociable way to de-stress (e.g., softball, basketball, tennis, boxing, soccer, golf).

Socializing—Having dinner or doing some other type of activity with friends or family (ones you like being with!) can be a great way to relax and refuel.

Entertainment—Watching your favorite TV show, seeing a movie, going to a concert, or listening to music at home can be nice ways to relax, have fun, and escape from the stresses of the day.

Video Games—Video games are not just for kids and teens anymore. With the advancements in technology and explosion in popularity, there are now a huge variety of video games for men and women of all ages and interests. It's a great way to relieve stress and to take your mind off of your worries.

Vacation—Taking a vacation is one of the best ways to decompress, because it takes you away from your daily environment, and puts you in a place where your only responsibility is to relax and have fun. The ideal vacation is one where you can get away from your phone, computer, email, and the daily demands of life, and be able to do, or not do, whatever you want. This can be an extended vacation to a far away land, or an overnight getaway to a cozy bed and breakfast an hour's drive away.

Pets—Taking the dog for a walk can be a good de-stressor, as it allows you to get some fresh air, get a little exercise, and spend time with your pal.

Hobbies—Engaging in a hobby you enjoy is a great way to relieve stress, because it allows you to focus your mind on something enjoyable, and maybe even challenging, which forces you to take your mind off any worries or stressors. There are hundreds of hobbies to choose from (e.g., woodworking, drawing, model building, puzzles, word games, coin collecting, gardening, fixing and rebuilding cars).

I've just scratched the surface here. There are hundreds more hobbies and leisure activities one can engage in or try out as potential stress relievers. All you have to do is choose some, try them out and see what you like, can afford, and can fit into your schedule, and then start engaging in them on a regular basis to reap the de-stressing benefits.

In addition to using hobbies and leisure activities as a way to manage stress, there are some stress management tools that everyone, male or female, young or old, should have in their toolbox. These include: time management skills, organization skills, prioritization skills, communication and assertiveness skills, sleep hygiene techniques, knowing when to take breaks, eating a nutritious diet, and thinking and problem-solving skills. There are many books and workbooks that can help you learn and apply these skills, or you can learn them from a counselor or therapist.

Steve Orma, PsyD

Does being very strict about a child's whereabouts and friends reduce the risk he will get involved with drugs?

It is very helpful to know a child's friends and to know where your child is at all times. As a child enters his mid-teens however, he may demand privacy and begin to hide his whereabouts and activities from you. Ideally, you will have created a relationship over the years in which he feels comfortable being honest with you. While being strict may be beneficial, you shouldn't be so strict or frightening that he is afraid to come to you with problems, such as coping with peer pressure to drink or use drugs. An overbearing strictness may lead to rebellion and worse behavior than would otherwise occur.

Talk with your child about drugs and alcohol from an early age and make sure he understands the dangers, such as car wrecks and death from intoxication, as well as understanding your moral beliefs about the use of illegal substances. If you suspect your child is on drugs or using alcohol, seek help from a mental health professional or drug counselor.

Lucy

Is it best to avoid dating someone with a personality disorder?

The American Psychiatric Association recognizes ten personality disorders: dependent, avoidant, borderline, antisocial, narcissistic, obsessive-compulsive, schizotypal, schizoid, histrionic and paranoid personality disorders. Don't confuse bad behavior or quirkiness with a true personality disorder. They are diagnosed when thoughts and resultant behaviors are serious enough to interfere with the development and maintenance of healthy relationships.

It is very difficult to maintain a healthy relationship with people who have some of the personality disorders. If you're the type of person who wouldn't want to be married to a narcissist, you probably shouldn't date one, either. It is possible to have a healthy relationship with someone with a personality disorder, but you must fully understand the disorder and he must be actively working on developing healthy coping and interpersonal skills. It may be fairly easy to get along with someone with obsessive-compulsive personality disorder, for example, but someone with schizoid, schizotypal or paranoid personality disorder may be very hard to understand. Some people with antisocial or borderline personality disorder can be downright dangerous at times, especially if you attempt to end the relationship. People don't come with warning labels, so if someone you date begins to show signs of a personality disorder, take it as a sign that you should encourage them to seek help. Be aware that personality disorders can be very difficult to treat and that the person must be motivated to change their behavior and way of looking at the world. On the other hand, millions of Americans have personality disorders and many of them manage to maintain healthy relationships, so don't be disheartened if you find yourself in love with one of them.

Lucy

Is it alright to try to get someone to remain in an intimate relationship if they want to leave?

If an intimate partner wants to leave, it is best to let them go. Begging them to stay only demeans you and creates an unhealthy dynamic, should you convince the person to remain. Truly, you don't want to be with someone who doesn't want to be with you and is only around out of a sense of guilt or responsibility. Healthy relationships are borne of love, mutual respect and a mutual desire to share life together. Allowing someone to go helps them realize their priorities and, sometimes, they will return. Regardless, you are better off sharing your time only with someone who truly wants to be there.

Lucy

What is the difference between a child who goes through a phase of being afraid of the dark and one who remains afraid of the dark for the rest of their lives?

Most children experience some fear of the dark; this fear seems to be inborn, as it is common across cultures and races. It is hypothesized that this fear is evolutionary, as many predators hunt at night. This fear generally begins around age 2-3, and lasts throughout most of childhood. In fact, the fear of darkness continues to be in the top ten fears for adults.

However, this fear becomes a mental health problem when the fear significantly disrupts daily living or daily activities. A typical fear of the dark might cause a child to occasionally call parents to their room in the middle of the night, avoid completely dark rooms (e.g., the basement), or ask parents to check dark spaces before they are able to feel completely safe. A more extreme fear presentation might be a child who absolutely refuses to be in semi-dark areas, even with parents or peers, or continues to worry about the dark even when parents or adults assure them that they are safe. When the fear of the dark disrupts the child's sleep, emotional stability, or ability to participate in activities around the house in an independent manner, professional psychological treatment may be indicated.

Nyctophobia, or the fear of the dark, can be crippling in adulthood. Adults who continue to be fearful of the dark may sleep with a nightlight, avoid entering dark rooms, and avoid being outside at night. Anxiety concerning the dark may result in symptoms such as increased heart rate, sweating, nausea, shaking, and panicked thoughts.

It is difficult to predict which children will leave the fear of the dark behind as a developmental phase, and which will develop a more intense adult fear of the dark. Those who are temperamentally anxious or have a family history of anxiety are at increased risk. If the fear of the dark becomes debilitating in childhood, professional treatment with an experienced psychologist is recommended; cognitive behavioral therapy (CBT) has been shown to be quite successful in resolving fears, anxieties, and phobias. Treatment in childhood can greatly reduce the likelihood that these fears will continue into adulthood.

Aimee Kotrba, PhD

Is there an easy way for a teacher to tell if a child is selectively mute rather than having an autism spectrum disorder?

Selective mutism is a childhood anxiety disorder characterized by avoidance of speaking in public, particularly in the school setting. These children can speak normally at home, but in school are either completely silent or demonstrate significant anxiety surrounding communication (both verbal and nonverbal). Because of the anxious symptoms of this selective mutism (e.g., poor eye contact, awkward/stiff movements, blank facial expression and lack of communication and speech), these children can look somewhat autistic in their presentation.

The defining characteristic between autism and selective mutism is the ability to speak normally in comfortable situations, such as the home setting. The parents of children with selective mutism report that their children are quite typical, talkative, and even bossy in the home setting, while children with autism often have expressive language difficulties and social skill weaknesses across settings (e.g., home, school, and in public). Thus, children with selective mutism almost have "two personalities" – the anxious, withdrawn, quiet presentation when the child is in a public setting, such as in school, at a restaurant, or in a peer activity such as Girl Scouts, and the talkative, outgoing, anxiety-free presentation in comfortable settings, such as at home or at a good friend's house.

The best way to assess for selective mutism is to obtain the parent's report on their child's ability to speak and socialize under comfortable situations that cause little anxiety, such as in their own home or in the home of a close friend. Parents tend to be accurate reporters of social skills and language abilities; thus, if parents see the child as typical in comfortable settings but quite anxious in social and academic settings, selective mutism should be considered. Furthermore, a videotape or audiotape of the child in the home environment is often helpful for teachers to see, as it provides a record of the child's social and verbal skills under optimal settings. Since children with selective mutism often become anxious and may act differently if they are aware that they are being videotaped, this may need to be done without the child's knowledge.

Selective mutism is treatable with behavioral psychotherapy and early intervention is key, so it is very important that teachers and pediatricians identify possible cases of selective mutism, and recommend that the child be evaluated by an experienced psychologist. More information about selective mutism can be found at www.selectivemutismtreatment.com or www.selectivemutism.org.

Aimee Kotrba, PhD

My relative has schizoaffective disorder. She doesn't trust us or want to be around us. How can I help her?

Schizoaffective disorder is a psychotic disorder that can lead to a lack of trust in others. Try not to take this personally and recognize that your relative would benefit from family contact, even if she seems to not trust you. It is best to go see her with a good attitude and let her know at least a few hours in advance that you plan to visit. Try not to ask too many questions, just tell her how you've been and the latest family news. Engaging in an activity such as taking a walk or preparing a meal may be a pleasant experience. Tell her you've enjoyed visiting with her and invite her to your home from time to time, but don't become upset if she doesn't come. Someone in the family should try to see that she has regular medical and psychiatric appointments and takes her medication as prescribed. If family members are unable or unwilling to do this, a case worker may be beneficial.

Lucy

How is talking to a psychologist different than talking to a friend?

A psychologist is trained in helping you work out your personal issues and recognize personality or mental health problems you may have. In some ways, it may feel like talking with a friend, but, depending on the type of psychologist you talk with, he may give you suggestions for new ways to think about the situations in your life, prescribe you treatment such as standing up for yourself or facing a phobia, or ask you questions that lead you to see your life in a much different way. A psychologist may help you explore how childhood trauma is affecting your day-to-day decisions or why you keep sabotaging yourself or how you can defeat addiction. Unlike friends, you can be assured that a psychologist will keep your conversations private, unless your or someone else's life may be in danger.

Lucy

How do you know when you need to see a psychologist?

Treatment with a psychologist is generally a decision that is based on several factors. The factors include the degree to which psychological problems are interfering with normal daily activities, career aspirations or the ability to function in the various roles that that individual has, e.g., parent, spouse, student, employee/employer. Many individuals seek some form of therapy to help them with life adjustment problems such as divorce, retirement, graduation or other status changes. These changes can bring on varying degrees of depression, anxiety, and sleep and eating disturbances that may cause major problems in interpersonal relationships or in daily functioning.

Does everyone who seeks the help of a psychologist have a psychiatric disorder? I ask this because many people have the mistaken idea that only those with true psychiatric disorders go into therapy. They are fearful that people will think they're "crazy" or that they will be hospitalized against their will. It couldn't be further from the truth. Seeing a psychologist is a positive step in the direction of helping yourself lead a more self-directed life of fulfillment and satisfaction. It doesn't mean you will be in therapy for years because many things can be handled within a relatively short period of time.

So, when you feel you can no longer handle what life is presenting to you and the quality of your life has degraded to the point that you feel you need help, it's a good idea to have a consultation with a psychologist. You don't have to be totally incapable of functioning, but you will have noticed a disturbing difference in the way you face the requirements of daily living. Your first step, of course, before going into therapy will be to make an evaluation of the problems you perceive and how you can handle them. When you note that you are having trouble finding solutions to these problems, it's a good time to consider the services of a psychologist.

Patricia Farrell, PhD

What should you do if you are afraid to see a psychologist because you view them as someone who can diagnose you as "crazy" or lock you up?

Currently, it is rather common for people to be in therapy with a psychologist. The media has provided a great deal of information on people who have sought psychological help and have benefited from it. Therefore, the stigma, which was originally attached to it, no longer exists, as we knew it.

In fact, the laws that currently cover commitment to a psychiatric facility do not permit anyone being committed unless they are a danger to themselves or others. Even when this may be the case and readily apparent, the usual course is that the person has to be seen by two psychiatrists who have to sign an agreement that the person needs hospitalization.

The days of casual, involuntary hospitalization are over and, in fact, hospitals are more likely to try to help people remain in the community rather than be hospitalized. At one time, husbands could have their wives committed to a psychiatric hospital for a very simple problem such as being irritable and people could voluntarily walk up to the admissions unit of a psychiatric hospital and have themselves admitted. Again, this is no longer the case. It is much harder to get into a psychiatric hospital these days and psychiatric hospital stays will be limited, in many cases, to just 15 days. Hospitalization is expensive and, although it may be helpful in some cases, professionals believe that living in the community and learning to deal with the problem there is actually more beneficial for the patient.

In order to help people to decide when they may need to go into therapy and how they might be able to help themselves prior to therapy, I wrote "How to Be Your Own Therapist" (McGraw-Hill). In this book, I also explain how to interview a therapist and what questions should be asked and answered prior to agreeing to enter into a therapeutic relationship. Framed diplomas or certificates on the wall are no guarantee that this is the person for you or that the person is truly qualified to handle your particular problems.

A second book, which I recently had published, "It's Not All in Your Head," deals with the psychological problems that can be caused by autoimmune disorders such as multiple sclerosis (MS). In fact, in my practice I always request that new patients have a complete medical evaluation prior to us beginning therapy. I do this because I know that many medical disorders can present as psychiatric or psychological disorders and I want those to be ruled out first.

I also maintain a website, www.drfarrell.net, where I provide a wealth of information on a variety of psychological subjects including anxiety, depression, panic disorder, self-help techniques and videos which explain some of the disorders. I believe that there is a great deal that people can do for themselves and I want to provide those self-help techniques to them free of charge. It's something I believe all mental health professionals should be doing in some way.

Patricia Farrell, PhD

Why do some people become psychopaths?

Psychopaths are called sociopaths today by the medical community. They have a disorder known as antisocial personality disorder, but they are on the extreme end. They supposedly lack a conscience but, in many cases, they will have one person or a small group of people they do seem to have feelings for and go to lengths to protect.

Like most mental illnesses, psychopathy seems to be a mixture of genetics and environment. You can envision that a psychopath thousands of years ago may have been a revered, feared warrior rather than landing in prison as many of them do today. In our society, we place value on getting along with others and having natural empathy. People who have empathy for others do seem to live happier lives than those who don't, and I do believe many psychopaths feel miserable much of the time. Some keep to themselves, but many wreak havoc on a small or large scale for much of their lives.

Lucy

What is OCD? I hear there are many different types.

Obsessive-compulsive disorder is an anxiety disorder characterized by unwanted, repeated thoughts that are temporarily relieved by repetitive actions. A classic example involves checking ten times to see if the stove is turned off. OCD fears involve things that could actually happen—it might involve a killer breaking into the house but not a monster attacking the sufferer. It can develop in childhood but is more common among adults. It is typically a lifelong disorder once in begins, although it waxes and wanes over the years.

As far as types, you may be thinking about hoarding disorder, which is considered by many to be a type of OCD. Hypochondria and anorexia nervosa have components that are similar to OCD. It is also true that some people are more obsessive while others are more compulsive. People with OCD may fear germs and wash their hands hundreds of times a day, have a need to count objects, recheck a letter dozens of times before sending it, worry they are going to hell or be afraid they have run over someone with a car. Part of their mind often realizes that the thoughts are irrational, but the extreme discomfort continues. Some people with obsessive-compulsive disorder become afraid that others have false thoughts about them, such as thinking that others perceive them as gay, snobbish, weird, or crazy.

OCD problems typically arise in one of three areas: the individual spends so much time performing compulsive behaviors that he cannot manage his life, he worries so much he cannot concentrate on his work, or he has fears that interfere with his relationships, such as believing his spouse doesn't really love him "enough".

Lucy

Why does addiction exist when it seems like something that is harmful to the organism? In other words, why do you our brains allow, or even encourage, us to become addicted to harmful substances? We don't get addicted to broccoli, for example, but to harmful drugs instead.

Why do we become addicted? Why does our brain allow, or even encourage us to become dependent on dangerous or destructive substances or activities? These are complex questions, as the causes of addiction include biological, psychological and emotional factors.

Understanding the interplay of all of these factors enables us to see how people can be addicted to obviously bad things, like drugs, alcohol and gambling, but also to less obviously bad things like work, exercise, food and sex.

Biologically, we have centers in our brain which mediate our response to pleasure. The dopamine reward pathway has been known for some time as the major brain area involved with addiction, but more recent studies indicate that the serotonin, glutamate and GABA pathways are also associated with the addictive response.

A brain pathway is a group of neurons, or nerve cells, which connects two areas of the brain and transmits messages between them. The reward pathways mediate the experience of pleasure by releasing into the brain the reward-associated brain chemicals in both "addictive" behaviors as well as normal types of reward-seeking, such as looking for and eating food and all types of sexual behavior.

Basically, when we engage in a rewarding activity, whether good for us or bad, the brain releases the reward chemicals and we briefly have the experience of pleasure.

There are conflicting biological explanations for why one person can enjoy the occasional cocktail while another turns into a full-blown alcoholic; one is the theory that, in addicts, the reward pathways don't release as much of the pleasurable chemicals into the brain. Theoretically, this drives people to compulsively repeat the pleasurable activity as they try to achieve enough of a reward.

While researchers are still sorting out the biology of addiction, clinical practice shows strong evidence for the psychological and emotional causes of addiction. One interesting fact is that many people who have one addiction also suffer from other addictions.

Many over-eaters are also compulsive shoppers; many gamblers also drink and smoke to excess; many drug addicts also abuse alcohol. Additionally, many addicts also have "hidden" addictions like compulsive food restricting, working too much or over-exercising.

We've all heard stories about people who've quit smoking and then turned to over-eating, and how ex-alcoholics are known to overindulge in nicotine and caffeine during the breaks of their meetings.

—

Since weight-loss surgery has come along, we've seen that many of those individuals who are no longer able to over-eat have transferred their food addiction to gambling, shopping, alcohol abuse or compulsive sexual behavior.

So, we can see that addictions are all, in fact, interchangeable, and that when one is no longer possible, another will take its place. This is backed up by the psychological understanding of addiction.

Psychologically, addiction seems to come from the powerful drive to heal emotional wounds and meet emotional needs. These wounds and needs arise from childhood experiences of loss, abandonment, deprivation or abuse. Depending on how severe these experiences were and how resilient the child was, the adult could develop an addiction.

Addiction appears to be a way that the psyche pursues fulfillment, soothing, and compensation for past hurts or losses. The addictive impulse is an unsophisticated, primal survival mechanism and therefore isn't a conscious, deliberate choice. Rather, it happens on a more subtle psychological level, as the wounds and needs are experienced as physical hunger, the desire for oblivion or an urge to fill a void.

The person unconsciously goes to the substances or activities that are the most convenient and accessible and those which have been demonstrated by their family or society to be nurturing and pleasurable, or highly likely to provide an escape from pain and suffering. These could be "bad" things like crack cocaine, or "good" things like working too hard.

One thing all addictions have in common is that they cause only a temporary experience of soothing or relief, and this, in part, is what compels the person to repeat the behavior over and over, in the hope that eventually, it will "do the trick."

We can't get addicted to broccoli because it doesn't activate the reward centers in our brains, but we certainly can be addicted to chocolate, which is good for us in small amounts, and likewise to any potentially pleasurable substance or activity, especially if the key combination of a defective reward pathway and a difficult childhood are at play.

Marcia Sirota, MD

Is there anything to taking a high dose of propranolol after a trauma to reduce emotional scarring from it?

Propranolol is a drug in the class known as beta-blockers, and is most commonly prescribed for the treatment of high blood pressure. It's also used to treat the symptoms of anxiety: headache, shakiness, rapid breathing and rapid heartbeat. Recent studies show that it can also prevent the symptoms of post-traumatic stress disorder (PTSD).

Propranolol works to block the actions of two brain chemicals: adrenalin and noradrenalin, the "adrenergic" neurotransmitters. Adrenalin, also known as epinephrine, is involved in the "fight or flight response" and is responsible for the symptoms of agitation and excitement we feel when this chemical is released. Noradrenalin, also known as norepinephrine, improves our ability to lay down memories.

Victims of trauma experience a variety of reactions and symptoms immediately after the traumatic event. This is due to the release of adrenalin and noradrenalin which occurs when the fear response activates certain areas of the brain: parts of the amygdala and locus ceruleus.

According to studies published by Bryant et al. in 2000 and Shalev et al. in 1998, PTSD more commonly occurs in those individuals who, for as yet unclear reasons, have a higher level of activation of the adrenergic neurotransmitters. This activation is demonstrated by the increased symptoms of distress at the time of the traumatic event; in particular, a very rapid heart rate.

The brain changes in response to trauma, resulting in long-lasting effects. Increased activation of the adrenergic neurotransmitters is believed to cause PTSD because intense symptoms of arousal, i.e., palpitations at the time of trauma, cause brain processes which lead to a greater future fear response (Orr et al., 2000), and the increased activation of noradrenalin causes memories to be intensified and more long-lasting (Southwick et al., 1999).

One recent study out of France (Guillaume Vaiva et al., 2003) demonstrates that when propranolol is given within six hours of a traumatic event and continued for ten days, the outcome is superior to a placebo for reducing the symptoms of PTSD, one month after the traumatic event.

It's believed that propranolol minimizes the likelihood of developing PTSD by preventing the arousal symptoms which lead to brain changes after trauma and by reducing the memory of emotionally upsetting events (Cahill et al.,1994).

The subjects in the French study were otherwise healthy adults recruited after they appeared in the emergency room following a car accident or physical assault. The 11 study candidates had all been experiencing a very rapid heart rate, indicating that they were likely to develop PTSD in the near future. Eight other people from the same ER who had severe palpitations after an acutely traumatic incident but who refused the propranolol were included in the study as the untreated group, for the sake of comparison.

In this study, a relatively low dose of propranolol was used. The average daily dose for the most common conditions being treated by propranolol (chest pain, tremor, high blood pressure, palpitations) is between 80-320 milligrams daily. The study participants were given 40 milligrams, three times a day for seven days, and then the dose was tapered and discontinued over the next three days.

The study by Vaiva et al. showed that in the untreated group, three out of the eight developed PTSD, whereas only one of the 11 individuals treated with propranolol did, which was statistically significant. These findings, therefore, indicated that a moderate dose of propranolol could be useful in decreasing the symptoms of PTSD or even preventing it from developing, if used immediately after the occurrence of an acute traumatic event.

Marcia Sirota, MD

Why do some teenagers cut themselves?

Cutting is a complicated pattern of behavior that can occur for several reasons. For some, it is a way of expressing intense emotions that they don't feel they can safely express verbally. These feelings may be rage, sadness or rejection. For some, cutting gives them a sense of control in a life in which they feel they have little control. Some teens cut themselves in order to get rid of a feeling of numbness; it shows them that they are "alive." Still others cut due to an abusive past, as a way of reliving the pain with the hope of dealing with it. It can become a strong release mechanism, leading to repeated cutting despite efforts to stop.

Lucy

What exactly is Maslow's pyramid?

Abraham Maslow was a psychologist who, in 1943, theorized that we can view human needs in terms of a hierarchy, or pyramid. The idea is that your most basic needs must be met before you can concentrate on meeting higher needs. Put simply, if you're hungry, it's difficult to worry about whether you're happy or not. Here are the rungs of the pyramid, from bottom to top.

1. Physiological needs – food, water, sleep, ability to use the bathroom, breathing and sex fall here

2. Safety needs – being safe from the elements and danger, and the ability to keep your belongings safe fall here

3. Belonging needs – the need to be loved falls here. This is where family, friends and intimate lovers can be found.

4. Self-esteem needs – once the basic needs are met, you can concentrate on things relative to your self-esteem. The accomplishments of your career, respect from others and sense of achievement fall here.

5. Self-actualization needs – many mental health professionals believe that most people never reach self-actualization. It is the pinnacle of the pyramid, the point at which you have creativity, acknowledgement of the beauty around you, a realistic attitude, lack of prejudice, and understanding of universal truth. It is the feeling of having reached your true potential.

Lucy

If you are living with someone who has hit you, is it possible for them to get treatment and never do it again, or should you always leave because it will only escalate?

It takes months, perhaps years, for a person who is violent and out of control to learn self-control, and that's if he acknowledges he has a problem. Once the barrier to physical violence is crossed, the violence almost always escalates. The safest thing to do is to leave, which will both protect you and your children, and also give him an experience of the consequences of being violent. If that's enough to get him to make real changes, and to get help, then after he makes the change you can renegotiate the relationship. In the meantime, you should get help yourself to understand how you allowed yourself to get into that position. Violent relationships don't start out that way-- it's a progression of behavior that is accepted by the recipient, like the old story of a frog in a pot of cold water that's placed on the stove. You need to learn to set limits, say no, and stand up for yourself. You also need to make you and your children more important to you than any relationship.

Tina B. Tessina, PhD

What exactly is an open relationship and what are the pros and cons from a psychological standpoint?

There are several types of open relationships--cheating, swinging, non-monogamy and polyamory.

* Cheating is a form of non-consensual open relationship--one partner is open, the other doesn't know about it.

*Swinging is sex outside the marriage without relationship. That is, swingers usually go to swing clubs, where they meet partners solely to have sex. Attachments are not supposed to form, but they often do. Couples can be swingers together, which means they go to the club together and split up to have sex with strangers. Or, one partner can swing alone, whether his partner knows about it or not.

*Non-monogamy is a negotiated arrangement between a couple ranging from "do anything you like, I just don't want to know about it" (which usually doesn't work for long) to "let's have sex with other people, but only under these rules" (rules can be: we only do it together, as in threesomes, or we do what we want alone, but we're honest about it with each other).

*Polyamory is open sexuality with the intent to form multiple relationships. Group marriages, threesomes, foursomes and other configurations can all be within polyamory. The intent is to be unlimited in loving, but honest, kind and caring to everyone involved. There are often varying rules under which couples agree to polyamory.

Of course, all of these intentions can backfire, and open relationships are very difficult, because of the emotional and relationship dynamics.

Tina Tessina, PhD

How should a parent decide whether to give a child medication for ADHD?

This is a very tough question. Medications for ADHD affect brain chemistry and may possibly cause long-term changes in the brain. I wouldn't personally give a child ADHD medicine to please a teacher or anyone else. If the child is truly miserable and a respected pediatrician or child psychiatrist has recommended it after a period of observing the child and obtaining a thorough history, I would consider it. Under no circumstances would I give ADHD medication to a child under the age of six. I would constantly be monitoring my child for side effects, keeping the dosage as low as possible and asking for frequent evaluations to determine if the medication can be stopped. Before giving the drug, I would explore whether the child has a learning disability, simply learns better by doing rather than listening, or has an undiagnosed medical or psychological issue. Each child is different and a seven year old who cannot sit still in class does not necessarily have ADHD; he may simply develop that type of maturity a little later than other children.

Lucy

Why does research show that people who have a spiritual life lead happier, more resilient lives; are there things that nonspiritual people can incorporate into their own lives to obtain a similar result?

I am not surprised by these findings. They are certainly consistent with my personal and clinical observations over the last thirty years and the information presented in my LA Times bestselling book, *Sacred Healing: Integrating Spirituality With Psychotherapy*.

People who have a spiritual life have different core values and different internal states than individuals who profess no spiritual beliefs or experiences. One of the most important aspects of a real and authentic spiritual life is the realization that one's true nature is eternal and a part of a larger consciousness. Individuals may vary in their belief about this force, be it God, Jesus, Buddha, Allah, Krishna, Mohammed, or a particular enlightened Master. The actual belief concerning the nature and source of this spiritual reality is not the most important issue. It is the actual experience of this spiritual source that solidifies one's personal beliefs and values. The actual states of love, joy, peace and bliss are not tied to or determined by outer reality or circumstances. This is one of the reasons that spiritually aware people are more resilient. They are not at the total mercy of outer circumstances for their happiness.

When I traveled to India many years ago I was surprised and moved to see so much joy and light emanating from those individuals in dire poverty and living on the streets in Bombay, now Mumbai. These individuals possessed nothing by our Western standards, yet they appeared happier than many wealthier Americans. The nature of spiritual realization results in a direct awareness of the soul, which is by nature love, joy, peace and bliss. One discovers this inner truth not by the acquisition of outer gain, but by the redirection of one's awareness to an inner reality that has great depth and wisdom.

Once the inner spiritual world is discovered, many fears disappear. Certainly the fear of death dissolves as the realization of the eternal nature of the soul emerges. Loss of any kind no longer has a devastating and catastrophic result because a deeper sense of identity, support, and security exists. Anyone with a real degree of self-realization knows that life is transitory and attachments ultimately lead to suffering. When consciousness is stabilized in the deeper Self, then outer forces have less emotional impact.

I have had three major losses in my life: my younger brother by six years and both parents. I was especially close to my father when he left his body several years ago. Grief is a natural state of the human condition. There are strong energetic cords from the subtle body that connect us when we have loving, bonded relationships. It is emotionally painful when these are severed. I felt the waves of grief roll through my heart and it was painful. After three months, I decided to take a week off and go on retreat in Hawaii. I spent four to seven hours a day in deep meditation and by the end of the week I was so immersed in Divine light that the grief process had shifted. Even at the moment of my father's death, my experience was different from those with only a worldly context and experience. His room was filled with a sublime, golden light that was very loving. His presence was tangible! I sat with him for three hours in deep communion with his soul. He was no longer in his physical body, but yet still present.

In my most recent book, Bouncing Back: How to Recover When Life Knocks You Down, I discuss the importance and power of a spiritual life.

There is an additional boon to a spiritual life — wisdom. Direct spiritual knowledge is a function of the soul through an intuitive process. It is possible to experience the interconnection within all life. This direct knowledge removes the sense of isolation and separation that most people experience on a daily basis. This sense of unity creates a degree of comfort and support as you realize that God is in your heart, and we are all in this creation together. The eternity of the soul is revealed, and most fears fall away — especially the fear of death. More important than mere comfort, this Divine presence can have a tangible impact on your life and help you in the most amazing ways.

Resilience become possible when we feel are not alone and experience a tangible spiritual force which helps us feel stronger and supports our every need in this human condition. Isolation, helplessness, despair and fear undermine our ability to cope with the changes and challenges of earthly life. It is possible to live with hope and happiness and recover from loss and personal harm when we are consciously connected to a greater spiritual force. Even personal healing from disease and injury is facilitated by this subtle reality.

Another important reality to consider is that spiritually aware individuals feel a sense of meaning and purpose in their lives. They feel connected to a larger community and are motivated to help others. The result is a sense of joy. We suffer most when we are totally consumed and preoccupied about our own happiness. Self-centeredness and selfishness does not bring joy!

The term "nonspiritual" is interesting because we are all made in the image and likeness of God. This does not change just because we have no realization of this reality. It is probably better to describe someone as "unaware" or a "nonbeliever" of these realities. If someone has no direct experience of these more subtle realities, not to worry. I believe that the desire to be physically healthy and emotionally strong provides enough motivation to a try a simple research proven method: meditation. The research shows that meditation will lower heart disease, increase job satisfaction, improve interpersonal relationships, and lower stress and anxiety. These are all positive outcomes for any life. In additional, as one learns to quiet the mind and internalize consciousness, other more subtle realities may emerge. It does not take spiritual motivation or desire to incorporate a little meditation and proper breathing practice into one's life. If one also spends a little time trying to help others, that will lead to a great sense of joy as well.

Ronald L. Mann, PhD

What are the symptoms of autism?

Autism can affect communication, behavior and the ability to learn. Signs of an autism spectrum disorder include:

1. Poor eye contact and lack of engaging with parents and others.

2. Delayed language and repeating the words of others.

3. Lack of interest in developing friendships.

4. Lack of empathy.

5. Flapping of hands and rocking, especially when stressed.

6. A strong need for routine, such as a desire to eat the same foods every day or put on clothing the same way each day.

7. Preoccupation with a type of object or a certain topic and lack of interest in talking about anything else.

Children with autism may develop language skills, only to seemingly lose them during toddlerhood. Others never speak at all, grunting or making other vocalizations instead. Children suspected of having autism should be evaluated as soon as possible, as early intervention yields better results. These children often benefit from a variety of therapies. Their families can be taught the best ways to interact with them as well.

Lucy

Should autistic children be placed on a special diet?

While it's normal for the parents of a newly-diagnosed child to feel panicked and desperate, it is important to stick with medically-established treatment. No diet has been medically proven to benefit autistic children, and the best diet is the one recommended for all children: a good balance of fruits, vegetables, milk products, whole grains, protein and healthy fats. It is usually safe (but likely useless) to briefly experiment with eliminating one or a few foods as long as no entire food groups are eliminated. For example, if you wish to eliminate wheat products for a while, make sure you are giving your child other adequate whole grains, such as oats, popcorn and barley. I have heard of individual instances in which a child's symptoms improved as the result of a dietary change, but I don't know that the child had autism rather than some sort of allergy or dietary issue. I have heard of many more cases in which parents radically changed a child's diet, eliminating whole food groups, depriving the child of loved foods, and spending resources and time purchasing and preparing a special diet with no benefit and possible harm.

Lucy

If someone has generalized anxiety disorder, does the anxiety really come out of nowhere or is it brought on by conscious or subconscious influences?

The central feature of generalized anxiety disorder is excessive anxiety and worry about a variety of events and situations that the person has difficulty controlling. While some psychological theories propose that the anxiety is brought on by subconscious (or unconscious) influences, other theories such as cognitive behavioral psychology acknowledge that anxiety is a normal emotion that we all experience, and only becomes diagnosable as a disorder when it is excessive, can't be controlled, and causes interference in the person's life. As a result, many cognitive behavioral psychologists would say that in the case of generalized anxiety disorder, anxiety is more likely the result of either an exaggerated response to realistic problems that are present in the person's life (e.g., financial difficulties, unemployment, health issues) or generated by worries about future events that are vague but possible (e.g., being the victim of a terrorist attack, not finding a life partner).

Simon A. Rego, PsyD

What kind of professionals treat mental health problems?

Psychiatrists are medical doctors specially trained in psychiatry. They may provide therapy and prescribe medications. Psychologists, in most states, have a doctoral degree in psychology, such as a PhD or PsyD. There are clinical psychologists and counseling psychologists, and, while the difference isn't huge, a clinical psychologist is likely better prepared to treat psychotic disorders. Psychiatrists and psychologists are considered the top rung of mental health treatment.

Psychiatric nurse practitioners and psychiatric clinical nurse specialists provide therapy and often prescribe medications, sometimes under the supervision of a psychiatrist. They have specialized mental health training in addition to nursing school and usually have a master's degree or a doctoral degree.

Licensed clinical social workers are social workers with training in mental health. They provide therapy and counseling and hold at least a master's degree. Licensed professional counselors provide counseling services for some mental health problems, such as substance abuse and grief issues; they also hold at least a master's degree. All mental health professionals have a professional license.

Lucy

What should a parent do if their child is overweight to help without precipitating an eating disorder?

In the midst of all of the media attention on an obesity epidemic, it is easy for all of us to get caught up in the frenzy. When we are constantly being bombarded by messages about our children becoming too fat and being at high risk for traditionally adult conditions like hypertension and type 2 diabetes, we can find ourselves operating in crisis mode, ridding our cabinets of anything we deem "unhealthy."

This crisis mentality encourages us to operate from a place of fear, but, unfortunately, operating from that place creates an environment that fosters stress and illness rather than health. Thus, the first key to addressing a weight issue with your child is to take a long, deep breath. We need to approach this situation very sensitively, and this means being calm and focused.

Before running to grab the burger out of your child's hand, you need to make sure you are clear on what your concern is actually about. Are you worried about your child in particular? Are you concerned that he will face bullying at school? That she will develop a weight-related illness now or as an adult? Are you worried that other parents will think you are not doing a good job? Whatever the case may be, it's imperative to do a good deal of self-reflection. Sometimes our concerns are rooted in our biases about weight and shape, or our fears about our own appearance and health.

If you are concerned that your child's health is in jeopardy, or just want to create a healthier environment in your home, there are a few key things you can do. The first is to focus on changing your own relationship with food. As most of us know, children and even teenagers are extremely perceptive, and there's nothing more important that we can for them than to model the behaviors we would like to see in them. If we can increase our own intake of fruits and vegetables, it will go much further than simply reminding them to do so.

The next step is to encourage them to add things into their diet. What we know from research is that a focus on restricting or eliminating foods does not work, and can in fact lead to really unhealthy views about "good" and "bad" food. Moralizing food choices is never helpful. Instead, parents can encourage children to add more fruits, vegetables, whole-grains, and healthy fats into their diets.

Last, it's important to create positive feelings around both food and exercise. Neither should be clouded with punishment, but instead should be discussed as opportunities to do something new and exciting. Try taking your child to a farmer's market to pick out fresh foods, look up recipes for healthy meals together, or invite him or her on a bike ride in your neighborhood. Making healthy eating and physical activity enjoyable is key to helping children incorporate it as a life-long practice.

Ashley L. Solomon, PsyD

Can a parent treat an eating disorder by tying a punishment or reward to eating behaviors or should it always be handled by a professional?

Until more recently, the commonly held belief was that eating disorders needed to be treated by a professional with little involvement by parents. In fact, the mid-twentieth century saw a movement toward pushing parents out of the treatment of mental illness in general, blaming parents (and especially mothers) for their children's difficulties.

Fortunately, the paradigm has, and is, shifting dramatically and the importance of parents in the process of treating these disorders is being recognized more than ever. We know that social support, and particularly family support when available, is crucial in recovery from an eating disorder.

However, sometimes parents are really at a loss as to how to help their ill child. Particularly when it comes to eating disorders, parents often struggle with how to best interact with their child, who has sometimes become someone that they hardly recognize. It is important for parents to understand that these disorders ravage both the bodies and brains of a child, and thus the personality changes that they see in their child should not be considered a reflection of their own parenting or as something permanent.

While parents are a vital part of the treatment, they cannot go it alone. They need support themselves to manage these difficult illnesses, and this can come in the form of working with a trained psychotherapist. Many parents who want to take charge of the illness themselves will find a clinician who can support them in doing Family-Based Treatment, sometimes called the Maudsley Method. In this form of treatment, the parents are the ones implementing the treatment and are being guided and supported by a clinician. FBT believes that parents are the best possible people to help their child succeed.

FBT involves several stages, and at the beginning the parents take primary control over their child's eating. The philosophy is that the child has been medically compromised and unable to make healthy choices for himself or herself, and so the parents must step in to steer the sinking ship out of danger. Over time, the control is gradually given back to the adolescent as he or she begins to recover.

During the process, the parents may choose to reinforce positive choices by their child by offering rewards or to try to decrease negative choices by removing privileges. The important point is that the parents are the ones to choose how to best help their child. It is important for the parents to feel in control, as they know their family and child best. If rewards and punishments don't work, the parents may not choose to use them.

In general, punishment does not tend to be as effective as reinforcement, and so I encourage parents to use rewards whenever possible. This does not always mean tangible rewards, but could also mean verbal praise or increased independence. When using reinforcement, it's important to highlight what the child has done well. In the case of eating disorders, a child might be praised for joining the family at a restaurant, something she hasn't done in months. A parent might let the child know how well he or she is doing and how proud the parent is of the child.

Ashley L. Solomon, PsyD

Is there a difference between nervousness and anxiety?

Yes, there is a big difference and it's hard to understand if you've never had full-blown anxiety. Extreme nervousness is the feeling that you cannot stand the situation you are in, that you want to run or somehow make it stop. It is the feeling encountered by abused children and adults. It can occur as you wait in the ICU to see if your loved one is going to live or not, as you go to the door to see who is banging on it in the middle of the night or as you await some horrifying fate. Everyone has nervousness at times. Everyone experiences a degree of anxiety too, but the full-blown anxiety of a severe case of generalized anxiety disorder, social anxiety disorder, panic disorder or agoraphobia is an experience you never forget. Your heart may pound and you may feel that you cannot breathe. You may experience a need to run to the nearest exit or feel that you are about to pass out or lose your mind. Adrenaline courses through your system, causing you to have a feeling you wouldn't wish on your worst enemy. You may feel extremely uncomfortable and embarrassed, something not typically felt during nervousness. A nervous person is relieved when a resolution is reached to whatever they are worried about, while a person with an anxiety disorder may quickly think of something new to feel anxious about.

Lucy

If the parent of a gay teen recognizes that the teen is being severely bullied at school despite interventions, how can they know whether to take the teen out of the school or leave him in the situation?

That's a very difficult situation and likely varies per child as to what the parents should do. Federal laws are getting stricter on the issue of bullying in general, so the school is legally responsible to protect your child from bullying. I would talk to the teen about how he/she feels about staying at the school versus leaving. I may take the teen to visit schools that have LGBT (lesbian, gay, bisexual and transgendered) support groups or are known for being more accepting of LGBT students. I might even encourage the family to contact the local newspaper about the topic if the teenager feels comfortable with this.

We need to empower kids to face opposition and challenges but the daily wearing on him or her from the bullying abuse is likely to cause more harm and possibly danger. I would explain to the teen that not everyone has been taught to treat others how you would want to be treated or to think of others and that, unfortunately, in our society gays and lesbians and transgendered people are still socially acceptable to pick on. If your teen is in a school district that allows you different school options, such as a "School of Choice" program, I would encourage the child to find a new school. I would also encourage the parents to contact GLSEN (Gay, Lesbian and Straight Education Network), PFLAG (Parents, Families & Friends of Lesbians and Gays), and The Trevor Project for guidance.

Matthew Clark, PsyD

What is the earliest age at which a person might realize they are gay or bisexual?

I've had four year-olds who saw themselves as the other gender. They told people they were a girl when they actually had boy parts. For these children this was not just a stage or a game. This was very real to them and they had felt this way since they could remember. Their parents attested to this.

Many of my gay friends and I knew we were different since preschool age. We began to develop "little crushes" on boys when the other boys were experiencing them towards girls. Our sexuality develops and reveals itself subtly throughout early childhood with both heterosexuals and homosexuals. An LGBT child often senses that he or she is "different" at a very young age. With the onset of puberty and sexual development, many adolescents start to realize that they are gay, lesbian, bisexual, or transgender.

Matthew Clark, PsyD

What do clients learn in anger management therapy?

Anger management classes empower people to control themselves by placing a gap between their angry emotions and their behaviors. They may also learn that anger, at its core, is often pain, rejection or annoyance. It may be the result of too-high expectations, a desire to control others and situations rather than oneself, or it may be that a situation that invokes anger actually touches on a topic the person is sensitive about. For example, if an abusive mother told her child he was worthless, he may feel enraged when his wife criticizes him for losing his job. Learning the patterns that cause rage and learning how to avoid unhealthy responses are two common goals of anger management. Information about toxic relationships may be included. Tools are often given, such as walking away, closing angry discussions and taking time to cool down.

It is a common misconception that anger management classes merely tell people to be quiet and keep their emotions to themselves but they are usually designed to help people express themselves in safe, healthy ways instead.

Lucy

In what way is psychoanalysis more beneficial to the patient than other forms of therapy?

Psychoanalysis denotes both a theory of the functioning of the mind as well as a method of treatment of mental dysfunction. In psychoanalytic theory, there are two basic assumptions: one, that a great deal of mental activity is unconscious; and two, that there is a continuity of thoughts--psychic determinism--which operates both when a person is "free associating" during an analysis (i.e., suspending conscious control over his trend of thought) as well as, historically, (i.e., that there is a connection between what went on in the person's past and what goes on in the person's present). It is important to stress that there may be no conscious awareness of these connections. These two basic postulates enable the analyst/therapist to organize the conscious mental productions of a patient during an analysis. A major goal for the patient of the analytic procedure involves the gradual increase in conscious connections between disparate events in the present as well as connections between present life and the past.

Regardless of the label given to a treatment we can conceptualize therapeutic encounters as falling within a broad spectrum.

At one end are "Expressive Treatments" or rather "expressive interventions," where the analyst/therapist promotes an elaboration of personal thoughts, memories, and feelings and fosters the patient's immersion in his or her emotional experience (regardless of whether one conceptualizes the treatment as focusing on intra-psychic issues and/or relational issues). Within such an in-depth experience, both patient and therapist are emotionally engaged, with the therapist, of course, modulating his or her emotional responses to the patient in order to maintain clinical boundaries. During this kind of treatment, among the various interventions, the therapist facilitates the patient's understanding of his or her motives, how the patient responds to and defends him or herself against unpleasant emotions, and how the relationship between the patient and therapist is experienced by the patient and by the therapist (known as transference/countertransference). Within certain theoretical orientations there is an attempt to understand the connection between the patient's transference feelings and their origins in important figures in the patient's life.

At the other end of the spectrum are "Supportive Treatments" or "supportive interventions," where there is an attempt to keep the emotional engagement within certain bounds and to avoid greater and greater emotional immersion. The therapist/analyst uses encouragement, reassurance, perhaps promotion of logical thoughts and reasoning, clarification and reframing of internal and external dangers, promotion of autonomy, and management, such as setting limits with explanations, education, and facilitation of understanding of cause and effect, thus helping with developing a more realistic appraisal of realistic aspects of life.

All treatments, regardless of what they are labeled, use a variety of both interventions. At one end, psychoanalysis utilizes more expressive interventions and at the other end, supportive psychotherapy utilizes more supportive techniques. Virtually all treatments have a mixture of both kinds of elements, to varying degrees.

In all of the treatments the approach can be one which is open-ended or one that is time limited — whether explicitly stated or implicitly motivated by either patient or therapist. In a technique where one wants to promote mainly a remission of symptoms, fostering expressive exploration may be contraindicated because it would undermine a quick return to autonomous functioning. In some patients, one may not want to open things up because one may feel that opening things up may lead to too much emotionality, causing difficulties for the patient.

However, in those situations where an in-depth exploration is warranted, a psychoanalysis can achieve greater personality modifications, beyond symptom change.

Leon Hoffman, MD

How can a woman become a better mother than her own mother was to her?

Many mothers, particularly new mothers, may feel unsure of themselves in their maternal role. They may come to believe that they cannot trust their own perceptions and cannot act on their own convictions. Their anxiety over mothering and child rearing can have a negative impact on the child's sense of security and competence and internal sense of well-being, and the development in the child of an internal sense of control and mastery over difficult affects (known as affect regulation). Rather than believing that over time only they can become the real experts for their children, many mothers retain the feeling that only other people, particularly "professional experts" or their own mothers or caretakers for their children, know the right answer to basic child rearing questions. These "experts" can often be seen as mother-substitutes. Other mothers are convinced that only their mothers are the real mothers and they are not. Thus, they constantly seek advice and try to find the "right" way to parent in order to achieve perfection in their child rearing and in their children.

When a woman becomes a new mother several themes emerge in her mind. Most importantly, she is concerned with the growth and development of her new baby; she begins to become more and more emotionally connected with her new baby; she insures that there is a support system for her and her baby (such as her own mother or mother surrogates); and she reorganizes her sense of identity as a mother (not just a woman) in order to facilitate her taking care of her baby and herself.

New mothers can be very preoccupied with their own mothers and can replay the relationship with their mothers with professionals and nannies who can become surrogates for their own mothers. New mothers need affirmation from their own mothers and the mother surrogates because, in their new roles as mothers, they experience a sense of helplessness and anxiety and have difficulty tolerating aggression, ambivalence, and conflict.

There are three factors that help new mothers address their anxieties and try to overcome the obstacle that they may have experienced, which, in turn, allows them to develop more certainty and confidence in themselves as mothers.

1. Create relationships with other new mothers.
2. Develop relationships with maternal figures who can provide support and affirmation.
3. Accept the fact that ambivalence conflicts, especially around aggression, are universal and that the goal of maturity and development is not to eliminate conflicts but find better ways to master them.

-and-

Remember that the perfect is the enemy of the good.

Leon Hoffman, MD

Is there a way to improve my mental health that I haven't thought of?

1. Eat properly. You need a balance of nutrients each day. The new MyPlate by the USDA can give you a good idea of how you should be eating. Eat a variety of colorful produce each day and make sure you eat plenty of fatty fish, such as tuna, mackerel and salmon.

2. Spend time outdoors. Spend time in your backyard or in a park. See how many animals you can spot. Do you see squirrels, birds, butterflies, bugs or chipmunks? Research has shown that looking at living plants and greenery is healthy for you and it is often calming. Choose active vacations in which you hike, visit the beach or explore new terrain. Make a point to spend at least half an hour outdoors each day and encourage your immediate and extended family and friends to plan spring and fall gatherings outside, rather than indoors.

3. Play! Adults seldom think of playing, other than video games, Wii, etc. Instead, find other ways to play solo and with friends. Swing at the playground, ride the rides that are safe for adults such as the carousel, and swing from the monkey bars. Play solitaire yourself or rummy with friends. Be silly with your makeup, hair and clothes. Make art using crayons, magic markers or paints. Sing out loud, laugh for no reason, and skip or run just for the fun of it. These activities trigger childhood memories, activate tension release, take your mind off your problems and give you new ways to express yourself.

Lucy

Contributor Index

This incredible group of doctors each took time out of their busy schedules to contribute to this project. Please thank them by purchasing their books, using their services and following their future work. This is the cream of the crop in the mental health field!

Jeffrey L. Brown, PsyD

Jeffrey L. Brown, PsyD, ABPP
Licensed Psychologist
Instructor, Department of Psychiatry
Harvard Medical School
691 Massachusetts Avenue, Suite 3
Arlington, MA 02476
www.DrJeffBrown.com
www.TheWinnersBrainBook.com

Madeleine M. Castellanos, MD

Madeleine M. Castellanos is a physician and board certified psychiatrist who specializes in sex therapy with couples and individuals. She has a passion for exercise, nutrition, and the natural functioning of the body and how these apply to a healthier and a more fulfilling sex life and life overall. To this end, she works teaching others the power of their own mind/body through lectures and workshops, and she joins all those MDs who want to change the face of medicine to focus on prevention and true health. You can read more about her at ReclaimYourSexuality.com

Matthew Clark, PsyD

Dr. Matthew Clark is a gay psychologist and director of The Clark Institute in Grand Rapids Michigan. He and his staff of doctoral and masters level interns treat children, youth, and adults. Dr. Clark courageously reaches out to the LGBT Community in a predominantly Conservative Christian area of Southwest Michigan. His passion is helping LGBT people who come from Fundamental Christian backgrounds and are struggling with their self-identity, coming out process, suicidality, and coping skills. Dr. Clark is an active Board Member for the LGBT Network of Southwest Michigan (LGBT Center in GR) and Gays in Faith Together. He is the co-leader for the Media Relations department of the Gay Christian? Yes! Campaign in Southwest Michigan. He is active with a variety of charities such as Saving One Life (teenage suicide prevention) and coordinates an Art and Wine night for LGBT Artists. He is often interviewed on TV and radio, and in documentaries on a variety of psychological issues including LGBT issues such as Growing Up Gay, Gay Teen Suicide and Bullying, Lesbian Mothers, and Transgender issues. www.theclarkinstitute.com

Patricia Farrell, PhD

Patricia Farrell, PhD, is a licensed psychologist in NJ and Florida, moderator of WebMD's Anxiety/Panic Exchange, former research psychologist at Mt. Sinai Medical Center, NYC, medical consultant for NJ Dept. of Disability Determinations, former member of the NJ Board of Psychological Examiners, consultant to corporations, doctoral-level educator, psychiatry preceptor at UMDNJ, and author of professional articles, USMLE prep courses, CE courses for healthcare professionals and books including How to Be Your Own Therapist (McGraw-Hill) and It's Not All in Your Head (Demos Health). She is listed in Who's Who in America and Who's Who in the World. Her website, http://www.drfarrell.net, provides information for both professionals and consumers. Dr. Farrell is a member of The American Psychological Association and The American Federation of Television and Radio Artists (AFTRA).

Jennifer L. Fee, PsyD

Jennifer L. Fee, PsyD is a psychologist in North Orange County, CA who specializes in helping people overcome crippling anxiety, fears, and phobias. She has co-authored and produced three CD's pertaining to stress and anxiety entitled: BE STILL, STRESS-LESS!, and STRESS-LESS! ON HORSEBACK. Her websites are www.visionquestpsychservices.com and www.anxietyhelpforme.com .

Joann Paley Galst, PhD

Joann Galst, PhD is a cognitive behavioral psychologist practicing in New York City. She specializes in reproductive health issues including infertility and pregnancy loss and is co-author of *Ethical Dilemmas in Fertility Counseling*, published in 2010 by the American Psychological Association,.

Joann Paley Galst, PhD
30 E. 60th St., Suite 802
New York, NY 10022
jgalst@aol.com

Nzinga Harrison, MD

Nzinga Harrison, MD
Physician
Board Certified in General Psychiatry and Addiction Medicine

Leon Hoffman, MD

Leon Hoffman, MD
167 East 67th Street
NY, NY 10065
www.theparentchildcenter.org

Leon Hoffman, MD, co-Director, Pacella Parent Child Center and co-Director, Research Center of The NY Psychoanalytic Institute & Society and Chief Psychiatrist at West End Day School, has been a psychiatrist for four decades and a psychoanalyst for three decades, and training and supervising psychoanalyst in adult, adolescent and child psychoanalysis at The New York Psychoanalytic Society and Institute. He is a Board Certified Adult, Adolescent and Child Psychiatrist as well as Certified in Adult, Adolescent, and Child Psychoanalysis by the American Psychoanalytic Association. Dr. Hoffman has extensive experience with children with social and emotional difficulties, their parents, and the educators who work with them. He was an Associate editor for the *Journal of American Psychoanalytic Association* and served on the editorial boards for the *American Journal of Psychoanalysis* and the *Journal of Clinical Psychoanalysis*. Dr. Hoffman has published widely in a variety of areas both for the professional and general public and in recent years has become actively involved in systematic empirical research.

Aimee Kotrba, PhD

Dr. Aimee Kotrba is a licensed clinical psychologist in Plymouth, Michigan offering expert consultation, diagnosis, and psychological treatment of anxiety disorders in childhood. More information can be obtained on her website, www.drkotrba.com or www.selectivemutismtreatment.com.

Gary W. Lewandowski, Jr., PhD

Gary W. Lewandowski Jr. Ph.D. is an associate professor of psychology at Monmouth University in New Jersey. Dr. Lewandowski's work has also appeared in numerous media outlets such as: *CNN, the New York Times, Philadelphia Inquirer, WebMD, Radio Health Journal, Science Daily, Women's Health, Marie Claire, Woman's World, Maxim, Cosmopolitan, Men's Health, Self Magazine, USA Today,* and *Ladies' Home Journal.* He is the co-author of the upcoming book *"The Science of Relationships: Answers to Your Questions about Dating, Marriage, and Family"* as well as the co-founder, editor, and writer for www.ScienceofRelationships.com.

Carole Lieberman, MD

Dr. Carole Lieberman, MD, MPH
Media Psychiatrist and Bestselling Author
Three-time Emmy Award Winning Host
Expert Witness
Author of "Bad Girls: Why Men Love Them & How Good Girls Can Learn Their Secrets"
www.DrCarole.com

Ronald L. Mann, PhD

Ronald L. Mann, PhD
Clinical Psychologist, Spiritual Teacher and Sport Psychologist

---

Samuel Mowerman, MD

Samuel Mowerman, MD
Board-Certified Psychiatrist
Voluntary Assistant Professor
Department of Psychiatry & Behavioral Sciences
University of Miami, Miller School of Medicine

Steve Orma, PsyD

Steve Orma, PsyD
Clinical Psychologist specializing in the treatment of anxiety
and stress
Provides therapy and coaching in the San Francisco Bay Area
and nationwide by phone
Staff Psychologist at New Dawn Eating Disorders Recovery
Center, Sausalito
Featured in *Women's Health Magazine*, *Marin Magazine*, and
MSNBC.com, among others
For more information: www.drorma.com

Simon A. Rego, PsyD

Simon A. Rego, PsyD, ABPP, ACT is Director of Psychology training and the Cognitive Behavior Therapy Training Program at Montefiore Medical Center in the Bronx, NY and an Assistant Professor of Psychiatry and Behavioral Sciences at Albert Einstein College of Medicine. Dr. Rego is Board Certified in Cognitive Behavioral Psychology and a Fellow of both the American Academy of Cognitive and Behavioral Psychology and the Academy of Cognitive Therapy. He is a member of the Board of Directors of the Anxiety Disorders Association of America, a founding member of the New York City Cognitive Behavioral Therapy Association (NYC-CBT), and holds leadership positions in the Association for Behavioral and Cognitive Therapies.

Karen Sherman, PhD

Karen Sherman, PhD
NYS psychologist specializing in relationships to self and others.
Offers workshops and coaching.
Author of "Mindfulness and The Art of Choice: Transform Your Life"
Co-author of "Marriage Magic! Find It, Keep It, and Make It Last."
For more information, www.drkarensherman.com

Marcia Sirota, MD

Marcia Sirota, MD is a board-certified adult psychiatrist whose areas of interest include overcoming compulsive eating and addiction, healing from PTSD and childhood trauma, and unblocking creativity. She works with individuals and groups, and also runs workshops. She writes and blogs on a regular basis, and has had articles published on various mental health topics.

Ashley L. Solomon, PsyD

Dr. Ashley Solomon is a clinical psychologist who specializes in the treatment of eating and weight disorders, trauma, and severe mental illness. Her research interests are in prevention of eating disorders and the use of media literacy in improving body dissatisfaction. She also has a special interest in the use of social media in recovery and blogs at www.nourishing-the-soul.com about body image, self-esteem, and recovery. She is active in the various professional organizations, such as the American Psychological Association and the Academy for Eating Disorders, and serves as a board member for eating disorder advocacy organizations.

Tina B. Tessina, PhD

Tina B. Tessina, PhD, www.tinatessina.com is a licensed psychotherapist in private practice in Long Beach, Calif. since 1978 and author of 13 books in 17 languages, including *Money, Sex and Kids: Stop Fighting About the Three Things That Can Ruin Your Marriage* (Adams Media) and *The Commuter Marriage* (Adams Media). She publishes the *Happiness Tips from Tina* e-mail newsletter, and the "Dr. Romance" Blog www.drromance.typepad.com/dr_romance_blog. She has written and been interviewed for many national publications. Online, she's known as "Doctor Romance" and is a Redbook Love Network expert as well as columnist for Divorce360, Yahoo! Personals and ThirdAge.com. She tweets @tinatessina and is on Facebook and LinkedIn.

Mentwab Wuhib, PhD

Mentwab Wuhib, PhD
Licensed Clinical Psychologist in New York and London
MindSuite Consulting (Founder)
web site: www.mindsuiteconsulting.com
Email: mwuhib@mindsuiteconsulting.com

www.ingramcontent.com/pod-product-compliance
Lightning Source LLC
Chambersburg PA
CBHW060938040426

42445CB00011B/923